GW00493920

Table of Contents: Switzerland in its diversity

We would like to acknowledge the help of various federal offices, trade associations and other organisations in providing the information in this brochure.

The publication "Switzerland in its diversity" is produced every two years. This edition is available in English, German, French, Spanish and Portuguese.

2009 / 2010 edition

NATURE

EXCITING NATURAL HISTORY

Switzerland's surface discloses only a small part of its colourful and varied natural history. At first glance the striking feature is that it is a young country from a geological point of view: Ice Age glaciers and their meltwater rivers, post-Ice Age running water and landslides have all characterised the architecture of the landscape. These forms were created between a few thousand and a hundred thousand years ago and they conceal a world that is invisible to the naked eye: under the surface formation, massive layers from the Tertiary Period (e.g. molasses in the Mittelland), from the Mesozoic sea (e.g. the Kalkalps (part of the Alps mainly composed of limestone and dolomite) and Jura mountains) and the even older mountain cores (the Alps) form the foundation of Switzerland which is approximately five hundred million years old.

www.swissworld.org

Switzerland - land-locked Alpine state and North/South transit country

There are numerous countries which boast many exceptional features and contrasts. In Switzerland the remarkable thing – and this is a fundamental characteristic of the country – is that pronounced differences in nature and landscape come together within a small area.

Geologically, Switzerland is complex. It hosts part of the Alpine arc which extends over almost 1'000 km between Nice in southern France and the Austrian capital of Vienna. Closely connected with the Alps are the Mittelland and the Jura mountains, the country's other two main landscapes. The Alps occupy approximately 60% of the country, the Mittelland 30% and the Jura 10%.

In addition, in the south, Switzerland extends as far as the Po plane, whereas in the very north and, consequently, on the other side of the Rhine, it extends into the Black Forest. Geographically speaking, Switzerland is home to the middle section of the Alps and therefore occupies approximately 20% of the whole of the massif. All of Switzerland's principal rivers - the Rhône, Rhine, Reuss and Ticino - rise at St. Gotthard. Switzerland is sometimes called the "water tower" of Central Europe. Each of the major rivers flows in a different direction. Their valleys divide the Alps into several main sections: The northeastern group of ranges includes the Alpstein-Toggenburg area and the Glarus, Schwyz and eastern Uri Alps. The northwestern Alps include the Vaud, Fribourg, Bernese, Unterwalden and western Uri Alps. The southern Alps comprise the Valais, Ticino and Grisons Alps.

The Alps are the remains of a complicated layout of nappe ridges made up of folds and groups of folds, which have been pushed on top of each other many times and worn away by erosion. Their average height is approximately 1'700 m; about a hundred peaks are just about 4'000 m high or higher. The highest peak on Swiss territory, at 4'634 m, is the Dufour Peak in the Monte-Rosa Massif. The core of the Alps is formed by old granite and crystalline slates, with younger sediment composed of a very diverse range of materials overlying these. The Alps show a rich wealth of forms of multilayered valleys, terraces, mountain ledges, passes, chains and summit corridors. All these forms were created by Ice Age glaciers. The foothills of the Alps on the northwestern edge of the mountain range are mainly

Some geographical data		Borders	
Area	41'284,6 km²		
Maximum North-South extent	220,1 km	Total	1'881,5 km
Maximum West-East extent	348,4 km	Italy	741,3 km
Highest point: Dufour Peak	4'634 m	France	571,8 km
Lowest point: Lago Maggiore water level	193 m	Germany	362,5 km
Highest village: Juf GR	2'126 m	Austria	164,8 km
Lowest village: Ascona TI	196 m	Liechtenstein	41,1 km

Source: Swisstopo

comprised of conglomerates. The highest peaks are situated approximately 2'000 m above sea level.

The Mittelland is a "by-product" of the Alps. Following the folding of the Alps and the Jura, inlets and lakes remained in the area between these two mountain ranges. The folding of the Alps brought with it intensive erosion, so that mountain streams transported large quantities of sand, gravel and scree down to the plains. Here, in today's Mittelland, these deposits formed new rock strata under enormous pressure, namely nagelfluh and further molasses rock.

During the various Ice Ages – the last of which lasted until approximately 10'000 B.C. – the surface of the molasses was almost completely covered by the moraines

Wine-growing in the Lavaux region on Lake Geneva. A typical example of the close proximity of mountains, water and arable land which is frequently found in Switzerland.

Some well-known mountain peaks, Alps and foothills of the Alps (Altitude in metres above sea level)		(Altitude in metres above sea level)	
Aletschhorn VS	4'193	Pilatus NW/OW[1]	2'120
Basòdino TI/I	3'272	Piz Bernina GR	4'049
Bietschhorn VS	3'934	Piz Corvatsch GR[2]	3'451
Blümlisalphorn BE	3'660	Piz Kesch GR	3'418
Breithorn (Zermatt) VS/I	4'164	Piz Nair GR[1]	3'056
Dammastock VS/UR	3'630	Piz Palü GR/I	3'901
Dent Blanche VS	4'357	Pizzo Campo Tencia TI	3'072
Dents du Midi VS	3'257	Pizzo Centrale UR/TI	2'999
Dom VS	4'545	Pizzo Rotondo VS/TI	3'192
Dufourspitze (Monte Rosa) VS	4'634	Rheinwaldhorn GR	3'402
Eiger BE	3'970	Rigi SZ[1]	1'798
Finsteraarhorn BE/VS	4'274	Säntis AR/AI/SG[1]	2'503
Glärnisch GL	2'914	Schesaplana GR/A	2'964
Gornergrat VS[1]	3'135	Schreckhorn BE	4'078
Grand Combin VS	4'314	Titlis BE/OW[2]	3'238
Jungfrau BE/VS[2]	4'158	Tödi GL/GR	3'614
Les Diablerets VD/VS[2]	3'210	Weisshorn VS	4'506
Matterhorn VS/I		Weissmies VS	4'017
(first scaled 1865 by Edward Whymper)	4'478	Wetterhorn BE	3'692
Mönch BE/VS	4'107	Wildstrubel BE/VS	3'244
Jura			
Chasseral BE	1'607	Mont Tendre VD	1'679
Chasseron VD[2]	1'607	Randen SH	912
La Dôle VD	1'677	Tête de Ran NE	1'422
Lägeren AG/ZH	866	Weissenstein (Röti) SO[2]	1'395

[1] Mountain railways to summit   [2] Mountain railways near summit

Sources: Swisstopo, "Seilbahnen Schweiz" (Swiss Cable Cars)

of the Alpine glaciers. Many lateral and end moraines have been preserved as high, long hills. Ice Age erosion and deposition have formed a wave-like landscape which, in turn, favoured the creation of lakes.

Today, the Mittelland, which is on average 580 m high, forms a wide band from Lake Geneva to Lake Constance. It has a much more pleasant climate than the Alps and the Jura. Not least because of this the Mittelland has become the economic "heart" of Switzerland. The economy, settlements and transport have all been developed particularly successfully here.

The Jura is an arc of mountains made up of ranges, valleys and plateaux. In general, it has a simpler composition than the Alps. Its average height is 700 m, but there are also mountains which are over 1'600 m high. The highest Jura peak at 1'679 m is Mont Tendre in the Canton of Vaud. The Jura has three different types of mountain ranges, namely the Faltenjura in the south, the Plateaujura in the north and the Tafeljura in the east. Like the Mittelland, the Jura owes its existence to the Alps. The effect of the thrusts resulting from the folding of the Alps extended over the Mittelland and created folding, for its part, at its edge – the Jura, a mountain range composed of limestone. The folds of the Jura have a fairly regular, parallel running wavy structure. The curving-up of numerous folds eroded, lakes and rivers left valleys and gorges. Those Jura rivers which flow to the Mittelland cut through the folds perpendicularly and created the transverse valleys typical of the Jura. These "ravines" made it considerably easier to open up the Jura to traffic.

Lots of lakes and rivers - thanks to the rain

Switzerland's position in Central Europe means that it partakes of the four main climatic regions of Europe, namely the oceanic, North European (polar), Mediterranean and continental climatic areas. In addition, the division of Switzerland into many levels creates a multitude of regional and local climates and also ensures that, overall, Switzerland receives plenty of rain. However, the precipitation is distributed very unevenly over the country. The average rainfall – measured over recent decades – is 138 cm in Montreux, 155 cm in Lugano, 163 cm in Schwyz and 270 cm on the Säntis. In Scuol just 69 cm falls, 60 cm in Sion and, indeed, just 52 cm in Stalden in the Valais Visp valley. In the Valais the low precipitation has repercussions on agriculture; as a result there is a particularly dense irrigation network in operation in the Rhône valley and in some Central Valais valleys. The very different levels of rainfall explain how difficult, even impossible, it is to make general comments about a "Swiss climate" – except that it is temperate in the Mittelland: the average annual precipitation here is approximately 100 cm, the average annual amount of sunshine approximately 1'400 to 1'600 hours, and the average annual temperature 8 to 10°C. In other parts of the country the type of weather is really varied regionally, with decisive factors being wind conditions and duration of sunshine, altitude and other influences.

www.meteoschweiz.ch

As a result of its position in the middle latitudes and its expanse both to the north and the south of the Alps, Switzerland offers a diverse range of climatic types and correspondingly different habitats. A marked temperature rise has been taking place for more than 150 years, which makes itself felt in various ways including the dramatic retreat by the Alpine glaciers (below: Glacier de Moiry on Grand Cornier). On the other hand, the last Ice Age ended, geologically speaking, "only" around 11'500 years ago and we are currently in a warm interglacial phase. Research is therefore also dealing with the problem of how much of an effect human beings are having on the climate and, as a result, the shrinkage of the glaciers. The question arises as to whether the trend might end in a subtropical climate like that which prevailed throughout the country approximately 20 million years ago, similar to that in today's Ticino (above: on the bank of Lake Lugano).

The biggest glaciers

	Surface (km²)	Length (km)
Aletsch Glacier VS	86,63	23,95
Gorner Glacier VS	59,73	13,50
Fiescher Glacier VS	34,21	15,35
Unteraar Glacier BE	29,48	12,95
Oberaletsch Glacier VS	22,81	9,05
Lower Grindelwald Glacier BE	20,84	8,30
Corbassière Glacier VS	18,31	10,15
Gauli Glacier BE	17,70	6,55
Rhône Glacier VS	17,60	8,00
Findel Glacier VS	17,36	7,80

Source: Glacier report, Engineering Laboratory of Hydraulics, Hydrology and Glaciology of the ETH Zurich, 2007

The glaciers and rivers are the natural architects of Switzerland. The rivers carry away the rock which is eroded by the ice shelves and deposit it as gravel and sandbanks in the lowlands or in river deltas (left). Delta landscapes often form habitats and resting places for unusual birds such as the rare and strictly protected little bitterns (right).

Glaciers

Compared with the other Alpine countries, Switzerland has the largest proportion of the entire glacial area. Today, the Swiss glaciers still cover approximately 1'000 km² and therefore almost 3% of the total area of the country. However, they constitute just a fraction of the glacial expanse during the Ice Ages: at that time the glaciation extended over almost all of present-day Switzerland, and in the east and west even extended far beyond today's national borders. Since the mid 19th century, when there was a high level of glaciers in Switzerland and the other Alpine countries, the areas covered in ice have retreated by more than 50% and the glacial decline is not only continuing, but has even accelerated considerably since 1985. The changes in length of approximately a hundred of Switzerland's glaciers are systematically recorded each year and have been, in some cases, since 1884. There are currently three glaciers which have also been having changes in their mass recorded for several decades. Water draining off many of the glaciers supplies the hydroelectric power stations' reservoirs directly.

Rivers and lakes

Switzerland shares three continental water systems: the Rhine drains 67,7% of the country into the North Sea, the Rhône transports 18% of the water into the Mediterranean. The water from the Swiss rivers which flow into the Po (9,6%) and into the Etsch (0,3%) also reaches the Mediterranean. The Inn drains 4,4% of the country; it carries its water into the Donau, which empties into the Black Sea. Much of the character of Switzerland's landscape is due, in particular, to its many lakes – there are approximately 1'500. The larger Swiss lakes are located at the base of the Jura (Lake Geneva, Lake Neuchâtel and Lake Biel-Bienne), in the Mittelland (Lake Constance and Lake Zurich), in the foothills of the Alps or at the northern edge of the Alps (Lake Thun, Lake Brienz, Lake Zug and Lake Lucerne) and at the southern edge of the Alps (Lake Lugano and Lake Maggiore). Over and above this, there are countless smaller lakes with natural and manmade dams, particularly in the Alps, the most beautiful of which include the Silsersee and

With Switzerland's high precipitation, water is an ever-present factor in shaping the landscape. The water supply is fed by both excess precipitation, by the reserves represented by the snow-cover and glaciers as well as by groundwater. As a symbol of life itself, moving water in particular never ceases to fascinate, as the picture of the Giessbach Falls above Lake Brienz shows.

The Karst regions and the moor landscapes in the Entlebuch rank among the most valuable nature reserves in Switzerland. The fissured rock formations have been created by water which cuts deep rifts and holes, so-called clints, in the limestone. Thanks to the typical aspects of its landscape and its flora and fauna, the Entlebuch was the first region in Switzerland to gain UNESCO recognition as a biosphere reserve in 2001. www.biosphaere.ch

Silvaplanersee embedded in the unique landscape of the Upper Engadine.

Most of the lakes were formed by Ice Age glaciers. They fill powerful "ribbon" basins which were left by the glaciers; at the lower end they are partially surrounded by rings of moraines. All the lakes of the Mittelland – from Lake Constance in the northeastern corner to Lake Geneva in the southwestern corner of the country – originated during the Ice Age. The lakes of southern Switzerland are older: Lake Lugano and Lake Maggiore were created from the gorges of fierce mountain rivers. There are few lakes in Jura. The fact that the subsoil is permeable or has faults in those areas where it is composed of solid rock makes the formation of lakes difficult. The Lac de Joux in that part of the Jura situated in the Canton of Vaud and the Lac des Taillères in the area of the Jura located in Neuchâtel are typical karst lakes. Their basins do not have any above-ground drainage; their water seeps away in the crevasses of the limestone, re-emerging at a remote location as a source.

www.swisstopo.ch

Conservation and environmental protection

Switzerland's land utilisation is divided into six categories: Approximately 30% of the total area is covered with forestry, 24% is given over to agriculture and 13% to Alpine meadows. The settled area (7%) and the proportion of lakes and rivers (4%) are smaller, and 21% of the area cannot be cultivated. **www.statistik.admin.ch**

With the exception of the last category the country is strongly characterised by the hand of man. The increase in population has resulted in a "lack of space" and, consequently, differences of opinion: Advocates of economic growth would like to utilise and develop more land, whilst other circles disapprove of this: they want to maintain the natural and cultural assets.

The Federal Law on the Protection of the Environment came into force in 1983. It is a skeleton law, with its implementation being the responsibility of the cantons. The most important protagonist in environmental policy at federal level is the Federal Office for the Environment (FOEN). It is responsible for the sustainable utilisation of natural resources (land, water, forest, air and biological diversity), for protecting man against the dangers posed by nature (avalanches, flood and earthquakes) and for providing protection against excessive impacts (noise, waste and polluted areas, etc.). The FOEN works in partnership with the cantons and other partners from economics, politics and society.

The current focal points include forest and climate policy, but no new forest regime is set to be introduced in Switzerland. Following the National Council, the Council of States also voted on 12 March 2008 against the introduction of the revised Federal Law on Forests, thus resulting in the withdrawal of the popular initiative "Save the Swiss forest". The 1993 Federal Law on Forests will therefore remain in force, and all of the efforts to secure the long-term future of the protection forest, to protect and promote biological diversity, to preserve the quality of both groundwater and drinking water, to promote the added-value chain for timber and to improve the profitability of forestry operations will continue. Irrespective of the law, the FOEN wishes to intensify the promotion of timber. Timber is a good example of the sustainable utilisation of natural resources. In addition, the promotion of timber can bring economic actions and ecological concerns closer together. During the fifties the prevention of water pollution and during the sixties nature conservation and landscape protection were legally regulated. The federal authorities and numerous cantons have adopted provisions which deal principally with the causes of the damage which has occurred.

The Nature Conservation and Protection of the Homeland Act of 1966 was supplemented in 1987 with additional provisions regarding the protection of the biotopes. Neighbouring moors and moorland of outstanding beauty and national importance are strictly protected. In addition, with the new Parks Decree, the Confederation is supporting the creation of national and regional nature parks, nature discovery parks and biosphere reserves.

The strains on the environment – and, consequently, the population's living space – are constantly increasing in Switzerland as well. The previous environmental protection measures are to be extended. In order to

Conflicting interests: some would like to use every possible way to increase electrical power production. They would like to meet the country's rise in demand for energy, but also prepare for a future withdrawal from atomic energy. Others consider nature conservation a priority; it should not be compromised, but wherever possible expanded. Which interests have won in the Grimsel (picture), the catchment area of one of the largest hydroelectric power stations in Switzerland, is still uncertain: some want to enlarge the dam walls, while others wish to guarantee the survival of a marvellous high-altitude moor with arolla pines and larches.

Ibex (left): These powerful animals with their horns measuring up to a metre long are extremely nimble climbers. Marmots (right): In the event of danger these funny animals disappear in a flash into their burrow or into an escape tube, which extends up to two metres underground. Their main enemies are the fox and eagle. In particular, young and carefree animals are in peril.

In the Swiss National Park – which is a Category 1 Reserve (highest class of protection) according to the International Union for Nature Conservation – nature is given free rein, man being very much in the background. With an area of 172 km² the region in the south-eastern corner of the country is Switzerland's only national park. The habitat of the flora and fauna, which boasts a large number of species, stretches upwards from the mountain forests over alpine meadows to the high mountain region. www.nationalpark.ch

protect the ozone layer the Federal Council has already prohibited the use of chloro-fluorocarbons (CFCs). Since 1 January 2008 the Swiss Federal Customs Authority has been levying a duty of 12 francs per tonne of CO_2 emissions on imported fossil fuels, which corresponds to approximately 3 cents per litre of heating oil or 2,5 cents per cubic metre of gas. No duty is levied on timber and biomass, as these are CO_2-neutral: when these are burnt the same amount of CO_2 is released as was absorbed when they were growing or manufactured. The rate of duty was decided upon by parliament and approved by the Federal Council. If emissions do not reduce sufficiently, the rate of duty will be gradually increased in 2009 and 2010. In the course of the Bilateral Agreements II (cf. Chapter on "Foreign Policy", "Switzerland-EU" subsection), Switzerland became a full member of the European Environment Agency (EEA) in 2006. It is therefore involved in Europe-wide studies, can help to develop environmental protection measures at European level and can coordinate its own activities with those of neighbouring states.
www.umwelt-schweiz.ch

Switzerland 1:1 800 000

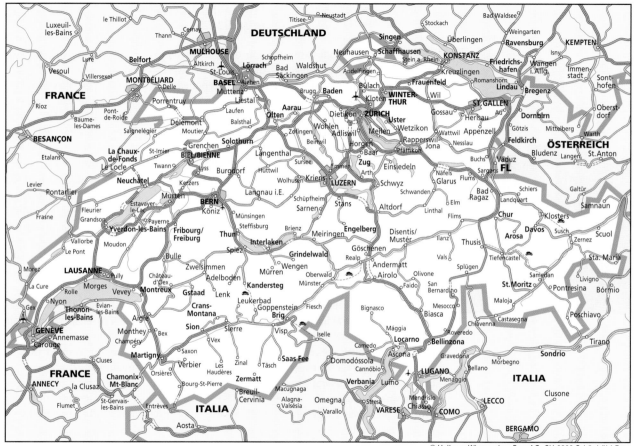

© Hallwag Kümmerly + Frey AG, CH-3322 Schönbühl-Bern

A POPULATED AREA SINCE TIME IMMEMORIAL

Various historical periods have shaped the Swiss cultural area, with the Celts, Romans and Germanic tribes having had the greatest influence. Between the hand-axes of the Old Stone Age and today's highly developed technology lies an eventful history – and constant growth in the population. The population of this small country is over 7,5 million. With an average population density of 186 inhabitants per km² - in the densely populated Mittelland it is in fact higher than 400 - Switzerland is one of the most densely populated countries in the world. The Federal Government, the Cantons and numerous private organisations are responsible for looking after the country's historical and cultural inheritance which includes, for instance, preserving the cultural heritage and ancient monuments.

www.swissworld.org

From migratory peoples to organised settlement area

The earliest traces of human activity which have been discovered on Swiss soil date back to the Old Stone Age. In the Cotencher cave in the Canton of Neuchâtel stone tools were discovered which very probably belonged to Neanderthal man, a distant ancestor of Homo sapiens.

The farmers of the New Stone Age – in Switzerland this covers the period from around 5000 to 2000 BC – brought about a decisive step forward in the development of the human race. This advance is also referred to as the "Neolithic revolution": for the first time human beings cleared and planted the land, occupied it continuously, so creating what today is described as a "man-made environment". Evidence of this period has been found at various places on Swiss soil; on the basis of piles it has been possible to reconstruct the ground plan of huts and entire settlements.

During the Bronze Age (2000-800 BC) and in the early Iron Age (up to approx. 450 BC) transport links gained in importance: mule paths were laid out in the mountains, thereby allowing trade to develop. Around 800 BC the first coins were put into circulation.

In the first century BC the Celtic tribe of the Helvetians leaves southern Germany, migrates into central Switzerland and further towards the west until it clashes with the Romans in eastern France. In 58 BC near

Bibracte, about 70 km to the southwest of Dijon, they are beaten by the Roman troops under Julius Caesar and forced to return to the Mittelland. From then on the area of Helvetian settlement is annexed to the Roman empire. This is an extremely fruitful Roman period, which gives wide areas of present-day Switzerland their first significant cultural transformation. A network of roads covers the country and cities grow up – among them the magnificent Aventicum (Avenches), the new capital of the Helvetians, and Augusta Raurica (Augst). Flourishing farming activity on large estates, typical of the Roman empire, leaves its mark on the land. In addition, the Romans bring Christianity to the country in the course of their period of rule.

The roots of Switzerland's four languages

Around the year 500, the phase of Romanisation comes to an end and Germanic tribes penetrate the country. As a result Switzerland is given that ethnic and linguistic structure which it still exhibits today. The already Christianised Burgundians settle in the western part of the country. They rapidly adapt to the Romanised population and even take up vulgar Latin – the direct forerunner of the Romance languages – which is spoken in this region. The Germanic Lombards migrate into southern Switzerland. They too do not interrupt the cultural development.

The Allemannians, who migrate into the area between the Rhine and Aare in large numbers, are in contrast still heathens. In the course of their occupation and settlement they advance far towards the southeast; their expansion is, however, halted by the Rhaetians. The latter are established in large parts of eastern Switzerland, the South Tyrol and Friulia, until they are forced back in the course of the Middle Ages; in Switzerland to the high valleys of Grisons, where they lead an independent life. It is the Rhaetians' admirable will to survive that one must thank for the fact that their language did not become absorbed into the neighbouring "major" languages, but was preserved. These events provide the foundation for the existence of four languages in Switzerland today: in the Romanesque or Burgundian west the transition from vulgar Latin to

The picture shows the remains of a Roman oven in Avenches used for baking bricks. The remains of several cultures can sometimes be found in one location, with objects superimposing themselves on one another in layers of earth.

The fortifications of Bellinzona rank among the most important testimonies to defensive construction in Switzerland. They form the sole remaining example of medieval military architecture in the whole of the Alpine region. The three castles Castelgrande (picture), Montebello and Sasso Corbaro were at one time all linked together by the Murata fortress wall. It was the special position of Bellinzona in the narrow point of the valley, with a number of alpine passes in the north and Italy in the south, which dictated that the fortresses be constructed. Begun by the Romans, the fortifications were extended by the Dukes of Milan in the 15th century to make them an almost impregnable fortress.

Franco-Provençal takes place. In what is today German-speaking Switzerland, the Alemannic language prevails in about 900, while in the south it is the Lombard dialects of Italian, in Grisons finally the Rhaeto-Romanic language.

Land occupation and settlement in the Middle Ages

In the Middle Ages nobility and clergy are essentially engaged in enriching and reshaping the cultural landscape. Imposing fortresses, castles and monasteries arise, and between the 9th and 14th centuries one city after another is founded. Among the rare evidence of the Carolingian period (8th-9th centuries) are the frescos in the church of the monastery of St. John the Baptist in Müstair (Grisons). The Cluniac abbeys of Romainmôtier and Payerne in the Canton of Vaud (10th century), the Great Minster in Zurich, and the minsters in Basle and Schaffhausen are the most important Romanesque buildings in Switzerland. The small church of St. Martin in Zillis (Grisons) contains a special treasure: the oldest surviving completely painted wooden ceiling

from around 1160 with 153 separate panels, depicting scenes from the life of Christ and of St. Martin. Later the Gothic style will characterise both church and lay buildings throughout Switzerland. Outstanding examples are the cathedrals in Lausanne and Geneva, and the minsters in Berne and Basle. The old town in Fribourg is an excellent example of a completely preserved Gothic town-plan. Not only the architecture, but also environment and living space were changed in this period. The nobility made a decisive contribution to causing the population to expand into previously unoccupied areas, for example into the upper Emmental, the Tösstal, the Appenzell, and into parts of the Jura and the Alps. In the course of this land occupation large areas of forest are cleared, and the land thus gained put into cultivation. At about the same time, the inhabitants of the upper Valais migrated towards the south and east. In around 1200 AD they set out to found colonies on the southern side of the Alps, in the Urserental, on the lower southern slopes of Monte-Rosa, in Grisons and in the Voralberg. They take possession of the previously uninhabited upper valleys. As a result in the Middle

Ages the settled area has already reached the extent which it occupies today. In the 12th century the Gotthard pass is opened to traffic – central Switzerland emerges from its isolation in respect of road links. Until then the Grisons passes and the Grand St. Bernard were the only Swiss alpine crossings.

Urbanisation and urban sprawl

The industrialisation of the 19th century brought about the most far-reaching change to the landscape to date. The industrialisation led to the modernisation of the infrastructure of the cities, which had an effect both on the environment and the people's living space. The cities grew beyond their walls and blurred the differences between town and country to a previously unheard-of extent. During the course of this, valuable cultural assets – primarily buildings and historic settlements – were adversely affected.

Cultural assets

The cultural inheritance, as shown in the evidence of history and in the landscape, must be looked after carefully. The stock of

Spiez Castle on Lake Thun. The lower part of the main tower (dating from around 1200) is composed of erratics, large boulders which were transported by the glacier. Over the years the castle has undergone remodelling by many owners with the result that the numerous building styles bear witness to the change from medieval fortress to patrician residence.

Fribourg, a town close to the linguistic and cultural barrier between German and French-speaking Switzerland, lies on a rocky ridge in a meander of the Saane. The medieval townscape remains intact. The largest protected old town in Europe has over 200 gothic buildings, as well as two kilometres of town walls and 14 towers.

The denominational split due to the Reformation and Counter-Reformation has characterised the cultural landscape right up until the present day. Religious art in the reformed Cantons is rather restrained. Following the Reformation Huguenot refugee families from France were involved in developing the economy in Geneva, and Zurich adopted a leading role amongst the reformed towns of the Swiss Confederation. In the Catholic districts, baroque masterpieces such as the St. Ursen cathedral in Solothurn, the collegiate church in St. Gall and Einsiedeln abbey were erected: the abbey church which is visible from a considerable distance is a splendid 18th century building, the magnificently furnished interior has been comprehensively restored in recent years (right).

The church of St. Martin in Zillis in the Canton of Grisons houses a treasure: one of the oldest, completely painted wooden roofs in the western world which has survived to the present day (left). 153 individual panels, dating back to the mid 12th century, portray scenes of the life of Christ and St Martin.

artistic and cultural monuments is extensive: churches, castles, town halls, stately homes in both town and country, historic city centres, whole villages... the most important are recorded by the Swiss authorities in national and regional inventories. As well as the classical historical and artistic monuments, these inventories also include culturally important buildings of more recent times (19th and 20th centuries) and, in addition, refer to the historically valuable gardens of the country. Looking after this cultural inheritance is the responsibility of the authorities in charge of preserving monuments. The Federal Government has been involved in this field since 1886, contributing both financial aid and specialist advice. In the last hundred years or so over 2'000 buildings have been placed under the protection of the Confederation. In addition, the Confederation supplements the efforts of the Cantons and communes in maintaining the buildings which are worthy of protection. Of the approximately 26 million Swiss francs which were spent in 2007 on fostering the protection of cultural heritage and care of ancient monuments, a full 20 million went to the Cantons, communes, institutions and private owners of assets which are worthy of protection. **www.kultur-schweiz.admin.ch**

One of the many organisations which are concerned with the care of cultural assets is the Society for Swiss Art History (GSK). Its primary task is carrying out scientific research into the architectural culture of Switzerland and making it accessible to the general public. The GSK presents Swiss artistic monuments in various publications. **www.gsk.ch**

Preservation of the Swiss farmhouse

Of all buildings, the farmhouse has been the most severely threatened in the last few decades. Whether concentrated in villages, as part of a scattered settlement or standing alone in the landscape, each farmhouse exhibits characteristic features which reflect its intended purpose – livestock breeding or agriculture – the climate and special uses. For a small country such as Switzerland, farmhouse architecture presents an amazing variety. To give only a few examples among many: in the Emmental the proud timber house with its hipped roof stands tall, in the Jura the wide, low stone house nestles down.

The half-timbered construction of northwest Switzerland carries a steep gabled roof, the wooden chalet of the Valais has up to four storeys and a brick-built kitchen, and on the large farmsteads of the Ticino the individual buildings are grouped around an inner courtyard. Following the example of other European countries, since 1978 an open-air museum has been working to counter the threat to the existence of the old farmhouses: on the Ballenberg near Brienz (Bernese Oberland) stand almost one hundred farmhouses from all parts of Switzerland. The buildings, typical of their regions and some of them hundreds of years old, were dismantled at the original site stone by stone, beam by beam, transported to the Ballenberg in their separate parts and rebuilt there in exactly their original form. The Ballenberg is thus an important contribution to the preservation of the cultural inheritance and at the same time a focus of folklore research in Switzerland. **www.ballenberg.ch**

Rescue measures

Cultural inheritance also comprises a huge range of different habits of everyday life, whether this is food and drink, clothing or "recreation": celebrations and traditional dress, religious festivals, popular art, music, theatre and dance, that is to say all traditional customs which are firmly fixed in society. In Switzerland numerous organisations devote themselves to looking after these forms of cultural presentation. Among the most important are the Swiss Folklore Society, over one hundred years old, the

The Swiss Open-Air Museum of Ballenberg displays more than a hundred historical farmhouses and ancillary buildings from the many different regions of Switzerland; the interiors of most of the buildings can also be visited.

In the Canton of Appenzell the Alpine descent is the culmination of a busy alpine summer. Wearing traditional dress, the proud alpine herdsmen and herdswomen lead their animals, which are magnificently adorned with flowers, back down into the valley.

"Schweizer Heimatschutz" ("Swiss Heritage Society") (founded in 1906), the Swiss Federation of National Costumes (founded 1926), "Swiss Traditional Crafts Society", which has been working on behalf of traditional Swiss handicrafts since 1930, and the "Pro Helvetia" foundation brought into being by the federal authorities in 1939.
www.pro-helvetia.ch, www.heimatschutz.ch
www.heimatwerk.ch, www.volkskunde.ch
www.trachtenvereinigung.ch

Festivals and customs

Most festivals are governed by the seasons, are related to church feast days or recall historical events. Whether practices which originally served to keep away evil spirits, sowing and harvest customs, "Alpchilbi" (fun fair) or New Year celebrations – all traditional festivals are deeply rooted in the rural population and, in addition, have the purpose of strengthening the sense of community.

Customs of the cold ...

Festivals are rather more common in winter than during the rest of the year: work in the fields pauses, people find more time for themselves and thus also more time to celebrate festivals.

On 6 December St. Nicholas' Day is celebrated in many places. For the "Klausjagen" in Küssnacht and Arth am Rigi (Schwyz) the "Kläuse" (St. Nicholas characters) are dressed up magnificently; as dusk falls the so-called "Iffelträger" parade through the town, with huge headdresses which are lit up from inside and remind the spectators of bishops' mitres.

Not until January, at "Silvesterklausen", do numerous "Kläuse" descend on the commune of Urnäsch (Appenzell Outer-Rhodes) with a noisy procession; their decorative masks show scenes from country life. On the Thursday before Ash Wednesday the "Roitschäggättä" (people covered in soot) wrapped in goat and sheep skins parade noisily through the villages of the Lötschental (Valais); with their demonic wooden masks their task originally was to frighten the evil spirits. The customs of the winter season are dominated by carnival. These crazy days are especially popular in German-speaking Switzerland, where they are celebrated in a wide variety of forms, for instance in Lucerne (with the "Fritschi procession"), in Herisau (with "Gidio Hosenstoss") and in Zug (with the "Greth-Schell" figure).

The most famous Swiss carnival takes place in Basle: for three days the carnival societies, called "Cliques", parade through the city in costume and wearing masks, to the sound of fife and drum.

Well-known festivals also ring in the spring: at the "Sechseläuten" in Zurich the "Böögg", a giant, straw-filled effigy which embodies the departing winter, is burned. On 1 March in Grisons "Chalandra Marz" is celebrated; the school children swing bells and crack whips, to drive away the winter.

... and the warm season

Throughout the country on 1 August the national holiday is celebrated to commemorate the foundation of the Swiss Federation in 1291, with speeches, fireworks, beacons and lantern processions. There are many mountain festivals, accompanied by folk-dancing, flag-waving, blowing alpine horns and the national sport of "Schwingen" (a form of wrestling). In the Gruyère region (Fribourg), in Appenzell Inner-Rhodes and Outer-Rhodes and elsewhere in the alpine region the herdsmen in old traditional costume assemble with their herds for the move up to the alpine summer pastures, the procession headed by the lead cow, decked with flowers. In the Lower Valais cow fights accompany the journey to the Alps, the winner then becoming leader of the herd. The important horse market in Saignelégier (Jura) is known as "Marché-Concours". However, the annual street parade in Zurich should also be mentioned. At the time of the grape harvest the vineyard festivals are celebrated, the climax usually being a colourful floral procession. The most famous are those held at Neuchâtel, Morges and Lugano.

Numerous historical festivals document the old Confederates' ability to put up a fight and desire for freedom. In particular, they are a reminder of important battles and feature processions with historic costumes and implements. Among the most famous festivals with a historical background is the Escalade in Geneva. Each winter the city celebrates its successful resistance to an attack by the Duke of Savoy with his troops in the night of 11 – 12 December 1602.

DYNAMIC COMPOSITION

As in many highly industrialised countries, the birth rate in Switzerland is relatively low. Today, immigration from foreign countries, particularly from countries and cultures with large families, has a greater influence on population growth. Two things are occurring: firstly, a shift of the residential population from city centres to outlying areas and, secondly, an influx from the country into built-up areas and secondary centres. In general, the last few decades have seen Switzerland continually undergoing social changes.

www.swissworld.org

One country, four languages

The Swiss Confederation has four national languages which are laid down in the Constitution: German, French, Italian and Rhaeto-Romanic (Romansch). This feature of having four languages dates back to the acquisition of land by Germanic tribes, which followed the Romanisation epoch. But today's language "boundaries" were not fixed until much later. Thus, the Rhaeto-Romanic language (Romansch) had already come under pressure from the Walser settlers, but did not disappear completely from the Rhine valley below Chur and in the Lower Prättigau until the 14th and 15th centuries. Elsewhere, the German-speaking Bernese Anabaptists settled in the French-speaking Jura between the 16th and 18th centuries to form solid enclaves of German-speaking settlers which are still there today.

Inside the main language groups one still finds many local dialects, although in French-speaking Switzerland, the Franco-provençal idiom has almost entirely died out. One occasionally hears it spoken by elderly people in certain areas of the Cantons of Valais, Jura and Fribourg; otherwise, French is usually spoken.

In Ticino and the southern Grisons valleys, the official language – Italian – is used for contact with the outside world, but in rural areas people prefer to communicate between themselves in the local Lombard dialect.

Languages

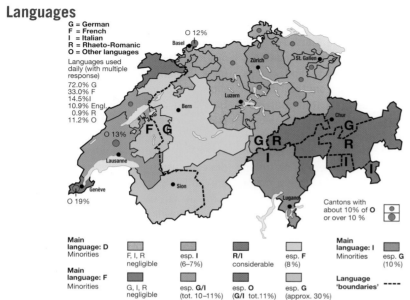

G = German
F = French
I = Italian
R = Rhaeto-Romanic
O = Other languages

Languages used
daily (with multiple
response)
72.0% G
33.0% F
14.5% I
10.9% Engl.
0.9% R
11.2% O

O 12%
Basel
Zürich
St. Gallen
Luzern
Bern
Chur
O 13%
Lausanne
Genève
O 19%
Sion
Lugano

Cantons with
about 10% of **O**
or over 10 %

Main language: D Minorities — F, I, R negligible | esp. **I** (6–7%) | **R/I** considerable | esp. **F** (8%)

Main language: I Minorities — esp. **G** (10%)

Main language: F Minorities — G, I, R negligible | esp. **G/I** (tot. 10–11%) | esp. **O** (G/I) tot.11% | esp. **G** (approx. 30%)

Language 'boundaries' - - - -

Population pyramid

Source: Federal Statistical Office,
Neuchâtel, (2007)

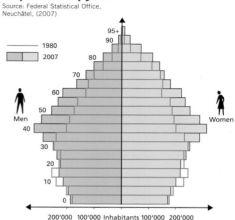

— 1980
▭ 2007

95+
90
80
70
60
50
40
30
20
10
0

Men   Women

200'000 100'000 Inhabitants 100'000 200'000

Distribution of population in Switzerland according to mother tongue

Year	German	French	Italian	Rhaeto-Romanic	Others
1950	72,1%	20,3%	5,9%	1,0%	0,7%
1970	64,9%	18,1%	11,9%	0,8%	4,3%
1980	65,0%	18,4%	9,8%	0,8%	6,0%
1990	63,6%	19,2%	7,6%	0,6%	8,9%
2000	63,7%	20,4%	6,5%	0,5%	9,0%

Source: 2000 national census

Demographic movements (‰)			
Year	Live births	Deaths	Excess of births
1900	28,6	19,3	9,3
1950	18,1	10,1	8,0
1970	16,1	9,2	6,9
1980	11,7	9,4	2,3
1990	12,5	9,5	3,0
1995	11,7	9,0	2,7
1996	11,7	8,9	2,8
1997	11,4	8,9	2,5
1998	11,0	8,8	2,2
1999	11,0	8,7	2,3
2000	10,9	8,7	2,2
2001	10,2	8,5	1,7
2002	10,0	8,5	1,5
2003	9,8	8,7	1,1
2004	9,9	8,2	1,7
2005	9,8	8,2	1,6
2006	9,8	8,1	1,7
2007	9,9	8,1	1,8

Source: Federal Statistical Office, Neuchâtel, (2008)

The situation is completely different in the case of Rhaeto-Romanic which acquired the status of the fourth national language in 1938. Rhaeto-Romanic is only spoken by a minority and comes under constant pressure from the "major" language groups (German, Italian) in surrounding areas. The number of people whose mother tongue is Rhaeto-Romanic is falling while the number of German speakers is increasing. There is no urban centre which could have become a major cultural and commercial centre as well, but, more importantly, the language itself lacks unity as it is formed of no fewer than five distinct dialects. The Ladin spoken by the people of the Engadine differs substantially from the Surmeir of the Oberhalbstein, or the Surselva of the Grisons "Oberland".

Obviously, this multiplicity causes problems in the struggle to preserve the Romansh culture and language. The State has increased its aid to this minority. If no action is taken now, by the year 2030, the Romansch dialects will possibly only be spoken by a handful of the older generation.

The widest variety of local dialects is found in German-speaking Switzerland. They are a geographical rather than a sociological phenomenon, and there are many more – and more individual – dialects than those of the major cantons, such as Berne, Basle and Zurich. The inhabitants of the isolated valleys are often particularly good at withstanding the test of time with their own, highly distinctive idiom. The German dialects used in everyday conversations are unlikely to give way to Standard German as used in official announcements as well as in writing.

Population growth through complex interrelationships

The growth in the Swiss population until the middle of the 19th century can only be roughly estimated. However, regular censuses since 1850 and annual records of changes in the number of inhabitants since 1980 provide an accurate picture of demographic movements.
www.statistik.admin.ch
The industrialisation during the 19th century created a lot of jobs and was responsible

for the first major increase in population. There was another big jump in population figures around the turn of the 20th century. As of 1940 there was a final significant bulge, with the population of Switzerland increasing by one third between 1950 and 1970.

After a period of slow growth in the 1970's (1,5%) the population of Switzerland increased again dramatically between 1980 and 2000. The rate of growth up to 1990 was 8% and 6% up to 2000. The increase during the nineties corresponds approximately to the population of the Canton of Geneva or the combined populations of the cities of Zurich and St. Gall.

The basic difference between the decades 1980 to 2000 and the previous decades is the dominant role played by the movement of foreigners. While the previous rise in population was mainly due to an excess of births over deaths, this aspect has contributed less and less to the increase in population since 1980. This trend was influenced by strong economic growth, especially in the second half of the 1980's. In 2003, the excess of births over deaths reached an all-time low of 8'700.

Total area and permanent[1] resident population early in 2008

Cantons	Population	Percentage of total population	Area (km²)	Density (Residents per km²)	Cantonal capital	Residents cantonal capitals
Zurich ZH	1'307'600	17,2	1'729	756	Zurich	358'540
Berne BE	963'000	12,7	5'959	162	Berne	122'658
Vaud VD	672'000	8,8	3'212	209	Lucerne	119'180
Argovia AG	581'600	7,7	1'404	414	Aarau	15'615
St. Gall SG	465'900	6,1	2'026	230	St. Gall	71'126
Geneva GE	438'200	5,8	282	1554	Geneva	179'971
Lucerne LU	363'500	4,8	1'493	243	Lucerne	58'381
Ticino TI	328'600	4,3	2'812	117	Bellinzona	17'111
Valais VS	298'600	3,9	5'225	57	Sion	28'871
Basle-Country BL	269'100	3,5	517	521	Liestal	13'245
Fribourg FR	263'200	3,5	1'671	158	Fribourg	33'836
Solothurn SO	250'200	3,3	791	316	Solothurn	15'364
Thurgovia TG	238'300	3,1	991	240	Frauenfeld	22'450
Grisons GR	188'800	2,5	7'105	27	Chur	32'513
Basle-Town BS	185'200	2,4	37	5005	Basle	163'521
Neuchâtel NE	169'800	2,2	803	211	Neuchâtel	32'664
Schwyz SZ	141'000	1,9	901	156	Schwyz	14'193
Zug ZG	109'100	1,4	239	456	Zug	25'486
Schaffhausen SH	74'500	1,0	299	249	Schaffhausen	33'693
Jura JU	69'600	0,9	839	83	Delémont	11'364
Appenzell O.Rh. AR	52'700	0,7	243	217	Herisau	15'282
Nidwalden NW	40'300	0,5	276	146	Stans	7'579
Glarus GL	38'200	0,5	685	56	Glarus	5'872
Uri UR	35'000	0,5	1'077	32	Altdorf	8'577
Obwalden OW	34'000	0,4	491	69	Sarnen	9'640
Appenzell I.Rh. AI	15'500	0,2	173	90	Appenzell	5'771
Switzerland	**7'593'500**	**100**	**41'280**	**186**		

[1] Swiss, foreigners with annual and with residence permits, international officials
Source: Federal Statistical Office, Neuchâtel (2008)

With their residential and industrial areas, large towns and cities are continually spreading out from the centre into the surrounding countryside. A clear example of this can be seen in Zurich, where the urbanised area is expanding along the lake (top). The number of people living in the city itself is falling. More offices and shops are replacing residential areas in the centre (bottom).

Since 2004, Switzerland has once more recorded a slight increase in the excess of births over deaths: in 2006, there were 13'405 more births than deaths. The rise in the population can, above all, be put down to immigration from abroad and is currently 1,1%.

Expanding urban area

With an average population density of approximately 186 inhabitants per km^2 Switzerland is densely populated. The settlement pattern is very irregular owing to soil types, with the majority living in the lowlands between the Jura and the Alps. Both urban communities and those communities located close to urban areas have seen particular growth, whilst the population in the rural areas – in the higher mountain areas and parts of the Jura – has fallen in part. Urban encroachment can be clearly seen by comparing the statistics for 1930, when only just over a third of the population (36%) were living in urban areas, with the figure for 2003, when this proportion had more than doubled (73%). Since the mid 1960's this growth has been concentrated on the smaller centres and the built-up areas: the population of the larger towns and cities has, in part, fallen considerably. Thanks to improved transport links, fewer regions have been "shrinking" in the last few years than previously. Overall, the number of people living in the rural areas in the 1990's even rose rather more sharply than in the urban areas. Most of the population live in communities with less than 10'000 inhabitants, with the majority living in communities with 2'000 to 5'000 inhabitants. At the end of 2005, 11 of the 26 cantons recorded a higher growth rate for their populations than the Swiss average (+0,6%), with the greatest increases being in the Cantons of Zug (+1,5%), Fribourg (+1,4%), Valais (+1,2%), Schwyz (+1,1%) and in Vaud and in Nidwalden (+1%). The population had fallen slightly in six cantons, for instance in Glarus (–0,7%) and Basle-Town (–0,3%).

Phases of immigration

The proportion of foreigners living in Switzerland remained low for many years; in 1860 less than 6% of the population were foreigners. The figure for permanent residents includes all foreigners with residence permits and all immigrants.
www.bfm.admin.ch

Number of Swiss people living abroad by continents and countries			
Europe	415'200	France	176'700
North and South America	169'300	Germany	75'000
Australia and Oceania	28'700	USA	74'000
Asia	35'600	Italy	48'000
Africa	19'300	Canada	37'700

Source: DFA Expatriate Swiss Service (2007)

The high rate of increase in immigration in the early 1960's, which was influenced by the economic boom, resulting in foreign workers being brought into the country, was attenuated through restrictions in 1963. At the end of 1960 there were 496'000 foreign permanent residents, representing 9,3% of the total population of Switzerland. The number of foreigners living in this country had risen to a record 1'066'000 (16,8%) in 1974.

In the following years a recession brought the upward trend to a standstill and was a major factor between 1975 and 1980 in reducing the number of foreigners by 120'000 to 893'000 (proportion of foreigners 14,1%). But then the trend changed once more. Although there was growth of only 47'000 between 1980 and 1985, this grew to 161'000 between 1985 and 1990 and 230'000 between 1990 and 1995. In 2007, the number of foreigners resident in Switzerland rose to 1'703'800. More than a fifth of all foreigners residing permanently in Switzerland were born in Switzerland and are second- or even third-generation foreigners. The proportion of foreigners in the total population has risen to 20,8%.

Regional variations in proportion of foreigners

The proportion of foreigners varies very considerably from one region to another. Depending on the degree of urbanisation, the economic structure and the distance from the national boundary, it fluctuates at canton level between 8,5% (Uri) and 38% (Geneva). It is especially high in cities and border areas which are also more closely linked with neighbouring countries from the point of view of regional economy.

These differences become even more striking, if we also include at least another 150'000 workers who regularly cross the frontiers to travel to their workplaces which are located almost exclusively in the border areas. The bilateral agreement with the EU on the free movement of persons is having an effect on the make-up of the foreign population in Switzerland. In 2005, the number of German nationals

Entry of foreigners according to reason for immigration 2007

Reason for immigration	Number	%
Subsequent immigration of foreign nationals' families	45'160	32,3
Foreigners with gainful employment subject to a quota	20'169	14,4
Foreigners with gainful employment without quota	47'439	34,0
Foreigners without gainful employment	4'930	3,5
Re-entries	92	0,1
Training and further training	14'628	10,5
Recognised refugees	1'154	0,8
Hardship cases	4'271	3,1
Other immigration	1'842	1,3
Total	**139'685**	**100**

Source: Federal Office for Migration (2008)

Foreigners permanently resident in Switzerland

	Total	Proportion of total population in %
1st December 1910	552'000	14,7
1st December 1950	285'000	6,1
1st December 1960	506'000	9,5
31st December 1970	983'000	15,9
31st December 1980	893'000	14,1
31st December 1990	1'100'000	16,4
31st December 2000	1'384'000	19,3
31st December 2001	1'419'095	19,7
31st December 2002	1'447'310	19,9
31st December 2003	1'471'000	20,1
31st December 2004	1'495'000	20,2
31st December 2005	1'511'937	20,3
31st December 2006	1'523'586	20,4
31st December 2007	1'570'965	20,8

Source: Federal Office for Migration (2008)

saw the greatest level of growth, followed by Portuguese and French nationals, while the number of nationals from Italy, Serbia and Montenegro, Spain, Bosnia-Herzegovina and Croatia has dropped.

Swiss abroad

Unfavourable economic conditions were for a long time the main reason why Swiss people emigrated temporarily or permanently. However, religious persecution, a sense of adventure and self-realisation were also important factors in the decision to settle abroad. The boroughs and Cantons encouraged emigration financially in the 19th century in order to avoid having to support the poorer population. Today, emigration for economic reasons has been replaced by individual and temporary emigration. It is mainly specialists who, for a limited time (under contract) or permanently, offer their skills to promote Swiss exports, cultural and economic cooperation or in research.

"The Fifth Switzerland" is the term used for the Swiss community living abroad. Today, there are more than 676'000 spread out over almost all the countries of the world. More than 70% of them have dual citizenship. Since 1966 an article in the Swiss Constitution has served as a basis for the law which applies in particular to the status of the Swiss residents abroad. Their interests in Switzerland are represented by the Council for the Swiss Abroad (ASO) in Berne and the Service for the Swiss Abroad which is part of the Federal Department of Foreign Affairs. These institutions also offer advice and other services to Swiss people living abroad.

www.eda.admin.ch/asd, www.aso.ch

The Council for the Swiss Abroad publishes the magazine "Swiss Revue" in five languages. It is sent free of charge to all Swiss people registered abroad.

More than 100'000 Swiss people living abroad take part in the political life of their homeland by post (i.e. in votes regarding Swiss bills and elections for the National Council).

Religion

Merchants and Roman soldiers spread the message of Christianity very early on in Switzerland. The first bishops were installed in Geneva, Martigny and Chur, but it was not until the beginning of the Middle Ages that the general populace was converted to Christianity. This came about partly through the efforts of the clergy and the aristocracy, but mainly through the teachings of itinerant Irish monks, such as Fridolin, Columban the Younger and Gallus. The numerous monasteries and convents were very active during a second phase of converting the populace to Christianity, instilling Christian virtues into everyday life. They all played a part in enriching the cultural life of the country at the time and monks such as Ratpert, Tuotilo and Ekkehart IV are especially remembered for their work. The Reformation originated in Zurich with Zwingli and radiated outwards. The Reformer was strongly influenced by the Humanism of Erasmus of Rotterdam. The new religion soon captured the imagination of all the German-speaking people, except for those in Central Switzerland. Those in the French-speaking regions and Ticino remained impervious to the new ideas until the region of Vaud was conquered by Berne in 1536. Others, mainly abroad, were converted through the teachings of Calvin in Geneva. Fribourg and Valais, however, remained faithful to their old religion. Because of the Catholic Counter-Reformation, the Canton of Solothurn, the Basle diocese and Grisons were only partially converted to Protestantism. In the Cantons of Glarus, Thurgovia, St. Gall and Grisons, the choice of faith was made at communal level, which explains the mixture of churches in these areas.

The freedom of residence granted by the Federal Constitution of 1848 introduced a considerable mix of religious denominations among the population. In addition, it must be mentioned that the Reformation and Counter-Reformation won through in part by force and Switzerland was ravaged by bloody religious wars in the 16th and 17th centuries.

Today, the Protestant churches are administered by a cantonal synod and a synod council. They all belong, together with a

In the middle of the 19th century almost 60% of the population of Switzerland was employed in agriculture; today this number has fallen to approximately 4% with workers having moved into manufacturing and the service industries. Farmers have always played an important role in shaping the landscape, however. The Swiss mountain village of Klosters is now making the most of this natural advantage as a typical tourist resort.

Despite the dense population in the lowlands and the constant growth of the built-up areas, Switzerland still boasts many unspoilt landscapes and recreational areas in the countryside. Away from the main traffic arteries and cities, an extensive network of hiking and cycling trails invites residents and visitors alike to explore nature.

Lugano is one of those cities which were built at the meeting point of overland and lake routes. In addition, this city also benefits from a picturesque location on the shores of the lake as well as a Mediterranean climate.

few free churches, to the Federation of Swiss Evangelical Churches. The Roman Catholic Church has six dioceses: Solothurn, Fribourg, Sion, Chur, St. Gall and Lugano. The abbeys at St-Maurice and Einsiedeln are both autonomous. The Old Catholic Church has just one Swiss diocese, based in Berne. There are also Jewish communities in approximately 20 Swiss towns, all allied to the Federation of Swiss Israelite Communities which was founded in 1904.

Denominations

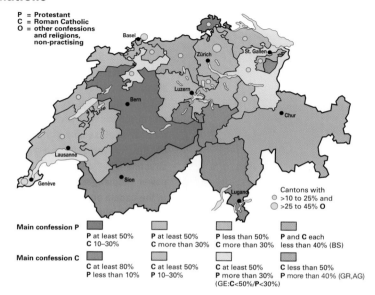

P = Protestant
C = Roman Catholic
O = other confessions and religions, non-practising

Cantons with
⚬ >10 to 25% and
⚫ >25 to 45% O

Main confession P

P at least 50% C 10–30%	P at least 50% C more than 30%	P less than 50% C more than 30%	P and C each less than 40% (BS)

Main confession C

C at least 80% P less than 10%	C at least 50% P 10–30%	C at least 50% P more than 30% (GE:C<50%/P<30%)	C less than 50% P more than 40% (GR,AG)

Distribution of population in Switzerland according to religion					
Years	Protestant	Roman Catholic	Old Catholic	Jews	Islam.	Other and affiliated
1970	47,8%	49,4%	0,3%	0,3%	0,3%	1,9%
1980	44,3%	47,6%	0,3%	0,3%	0,9%	6,6%
1990	40,0%	46,2%	0,2%	0,3%	2,2%	11,1%
2000	35,3%	41,8%	0,2%	0,2%	4,3%	18,2%

Source: 2000 national census

29

700 YEARS OF DEMOCRACY

Turbulent times have come and gone since the original oath was sworn on the Rütli in 1291. The decisive step from an alliance of states to a confederation came in 1848. Nowadays, the Swiss electorate has a direct or indirect say in all sectors of political life. Switzerland's federal structure with no strong central power encourages politics close to the people and establishes identity. In almost no other sovereign state do the people enjoy such an extensive right of participation, as do the citizens in Switzerland. The long democratic tradition, the relatively small size and total population, together with the high level of literacy and extensive media choice, are the vital factors for this particular type of state to function.

www.swissworld.org

Regional autonomy and living together at close quarters

The institutions and political organisation of 20th century Switzerland reflect, for the most part, the experiences of the last seven centuries. Methods of government developed more by a process of gradual change as the territory was extended, than by sudden upheavals or revolution. The co-existence of several regions with fixed boundaries in a restricted area has brought its own problems.

From the defence of primitive liberties in the 13th century – the major reason behind the alliance of the three valleys which formed the "core" of the Confederation – to present-day debates about the federal system, the basic need for regional autonomy has never been disputed. Because of its landlocked position at the heart of the continent, Switzerland has inevitably felt the repercussions of European history, although its physical geography has afforded it a degree of protection. The neutrality it has espoused since the 16th century made a substantial contribution to the protection of the mountain country from the outside world.

A brief history

The concept of an alliance of autonomous States was first mooted when men from the mountain Cantons of Uri, Schwyz and Unterwalden met in 1291 to pledge mutual aid and support, thus creating, almost unwittingly, the Helvetic Confederation. The alliance grew out of the desire to protect their traditional rights – self-determination and their own legal system – against the powerful Hapsburg Empire. Tradition has it that the oath of allegiance was taken on August 1st, 1291 on the Rütli meadow by Lake Lucerne.

The people of Central Switzerland then embarked on a series of wars to impose their law on the feudal territories of the Mittelland and to extend the alliance to other valleys and towns, forming first a Confederation of eight and then 13 Cantons by 1513.

This fairly loose association served in the first instance to defend jointly the independence of the individual Cantons and later to conquer and subdue new territories.

The political expansion of the hot-headed Confederates was brought to a brutal end at the battle of Marignano in the Lombardy plain in 1515. The political development of the country was then frustrated for some time by internal disagreements and a divergence of interests between the Cantons and European principalities – particularly regarding the service of Swiss mercenaries in foreign armies and, more especially, the religious problems thrown up by the Reformation. A prominent characteristic of the political situation at the time was the fact that the towns were governed by the local aristocracy and the rural Cantons by a democratically organised body.

The Confederates' decision to refuse to participate in any future European conflicts can be seen as their first step towards neutrality. This period also saw the end of the old Confederation. After the Directory troops occupied Switzerland in 1798 the unitarian Helvetic Republic was formed, abolishing all privileges and granting freedom of worship and the press.

In 1803, Napoleon put an end to the disputes between the federalists and those that favoured centralised government by decreeing the Act of Mediation, under which Switzerland became a Federal Republic composed of 19 Cantons. However, after the fall of the Emperor, the Confederation of States became once more – as it had been before 1798 – a fairly loose Confederation of 22 Cantons, and here and there, democratic rights were again restricted in favour of the aristocracy and the cities. It was during this

The three Confederates (from left to right) Walter Fürst, Werner Stauffacher and Arnold von Melchtal with the Federal Charter of 1291 in the entrance hall of the Parliament.

The domed hall in the parliament building. The glass dome shows the federal coats of arms of the 22 cantons. The coat of arms of the Canton of Jura is next to the others with the foundation year (1978) of the new Canton.

period, in 1815, that Switzerland's neutrality was recognised internationally.

From 1830 onwards, due to popular pressure, liberal constitutions were drawn up in 12 Cantons. 1847 saw the end of a brief civil war when the seven Conservative Catholic Cantons who had made their own separate alliance (Sonderbund) in an effort to preserve cantonal self-determination were conquered by the Protestant Cantons which already had liberal governments. This dispute resulted in 1848 in the foundation of a Federal State with progressive republican ideas, in the heart of a 19th century Europe made up of restored monarchies. The New Constitution was accepted in the same year by popular vote. It was totally revised in 1874 and has subsequently been adapted from time to time to meet new demands.

During the 19th century it underwent a change from an authoritarian state to a modern welfare state: a reconciliation took place, on the one hand, between the interests of the towns and the rural dwellers, on the other, between the various social strata. In 1967 preliminary work was started on a complete revision of the Federal Constitution. In 1987 the Federal Council was asked to prepare a draft for a New Constitution to be submitted to both chambers. After being adopted by the electorate and the Cantons the new Federal Constitution came into force on 1st January 2000.

Federalism

The Constitution of 1848, whose essential features are still relevant today, gave legal expression to the lessons drawn from Switzerland's history: the unity of the Helvetic State could only be preserved by respecting the individuality of its member states.

The Federal State today is made up of 26 autonomous Cantons and half-Cantons. The Cantons, as federal states, enjoy a high degree of freedom in their political decisions and administrative autonomy. Each Canton has its own constitution and laws: as do many communes within them. Of course, in many cases, the cantonal and communal laws follow the broad outlines of federal legislation yet still allow for particular local needs.

The duties of the Federal Government are strictly defined and laid down in the Constitution: it ensures internal and external security; upholds the cantonal constitutions and maintains diplomatic relations with foreign powers. Customs, the general provision of postal and telegraphic services, monetary controls and armed forces all come under its authority. It is responsible for arming the troops; creating laws that are fair to all (Code of Obligations, civil law, penal law); controlling the roads and railways, forestry, hunting, fishing and hydroelectric power. It imposes certain measures to ensure the continued economic development of the country (e.g. protecting agriculture) and its general welfare (social security, etc.). In many areas the Federal Government simply legislates and supervises, leaving it to the Cantons to carry out the legislation. The Constitution requires the Government at federal and cantonal level to take the form of a so-called semi-direct democracy. The Federal State is composed of the people and the Cantons, the Federal Assembly (Parliament), the Federal Council (Government) and the Federal Tribunal. **www.admin.ch**

Civil rights

Direct democracy means that the Swiss citizens are able to influence political decisions

Cantons: Growth of the resident population and representation in the National Council

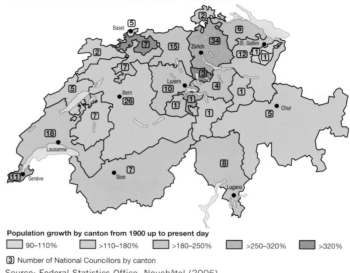

Population growth by canton from 1900 up to present day

☐ 90–110% ☐ >110–180% ☐ >180–250% ☐ >250–320% ☐ >320%

[3] Number of National Councillors by canton

Source: Federal Statistics Office, Neuchâtel (2006)

The fire and water services are among the many areas where local authorities are politically independent. The responsibilities of local authorities are highly complex today; for practical and financial reasons an increasing number of boroughs now fulfil certain tasks in conjunction with their neighbours.

to a large extent. All Swiss citizens are equal before the law, with each individual being settled in a particular commune. In addition, the Constitution explicitly guarantees freedom of private property ownership; freedom of trade and commerce; freedom of choice of domicile and worship; freedom of press; rights of association and petition. These rights are standard at federal level, but the Cantons and Communes may grant more extensive rights.

At federal level all Swiss citizens over the age of 18 can vote to elect the members of parliament and to decide on changes to the law and Constitution. Citizens are entitled to demand a change to the Constitution or law by means of a "popular initiative". In order for an initiative to come about, it requires the signatures of 100'000 persons who are entitled to vote to be collected within a period of 18 months.

The Federal Parliament is entitled to put forward a counterproposal and a popular vote is taken for both proposals. It should be noted that a double majority (from the voters and the Cantons) is needed for a change to be adopted. The main advantage of the right of initiative is that it incites political dis-

cussion. It gives the people the power to intervene directly in decision-making about legislation.

A Referendum can be either compulsory or optional: constitutional changes are subject to the Obligatory Referendum at both federal and cantonal level. The Optional Referendum enables the public to have their say about any federal legislation or general decrees. In practice, a minimum of 50'000 electors or eight Cantons have to request an Optional Referendum within 100 days of the official publication of any such measures. The Referendum is also practised at cantonal level, but the way it is used varies from one Canton to another.

www.bk.admin.ch
www.iri-europe.org
(Initiative & Referendum Institute Europe)

Cantons and communes

With the entry of the Canton of Jura (1979), the Confederation now comprises 26 autonomous member states, but only 23 Cantons, three of which are subdivided into half-Cantons. Unterwalden has since the 12th/14th centuries respectively been recognised as Nidwalden and Obwalden, Appenzell was divided into Inner- and Outer-Rhodes after the Reformation in 1597 and Basle was split into Basle-Town and Basle-Country when their civil war of 1833 put an end to the city's ambitions. The half-Cantons only have one seat in the Council of States and, in amendments to the Federal Constitution, their votes are only counted as half-votes. The Cantons and half-Cantons govern themselves independently. The citizens elect their cantonal authorities and take part in cantonal decisions. The cantonal government, composed of five, seven or nine members, normally elected by a secret ballot (except in the Cantons with a "Landsgemeinde"), operates along the lines of the collegiate system. The cantonal parliament – the cantonal Council or Greater Council – consists of a single chamber whose number of members varies greatly from Canton to Canton (between 58 and 200). The council members generally serve a four-year term with the following exceptions: Fribourg (five years); Appenzell Outer-Rhodes (three years); Grisons (two years); Appenzell Inner-Rhodes (one year). The Cantons, funded by direct taxation,

Largest (above) and smallest boroughs by km² (rounded)

Jura		Mittelland		Alps (foothills of the Alps included)		Southern side of the Alps	
Le Chenit VD	99,2	Zurich	87,8	Bagnes VS	282,3	Poschiavo GR	191,0
La Chaux-de-F, NE	55,7	Winterthur ZH	68,1	Davos GR	254,4	Mesocco GR	164,7
Arzier VD	51,9	Berne	51,6	Zermatt VS	242,7	Airolo TI	94,4
La Brévine NE	41,8	Köniz BE	51,0	Evolène VS	209,9	Bignasco TI	81,5
Ste-Croix VD	39,4	Ruswil LU	45,2	Zernez GR	203,9	Malvaglia TI	80,3
Mauraz VD	0,5	Kaiserstuhl AG	0,3	Pratval GR	0,8	Ponte Tresa TI	0,4
Stilli AG	0,6	Rivaz VD	0,3	Veysonnaz VS	1,1	Carabietta TI	0,5
Umiken AG	0,8	Gottlieben TG	0,3	Mörel VS	1,2	Muralto TI	0,6
Vaugondry VD	0,8	Meyriez FR	0,3	Lalden VS	1,3	Grancia TI	0,6
Kammersrohr SO	1,0	Paudex VD	0,5	Fürstenau GR	1,3	Gravesano TI	0,7

Source: Federal Statistics Office, Neuchâtel

have independent control over their education systems and social services.

Only Appenzell Inner-Rhodes and Glarus still retain an institution that is unique in the world: the "Landsgemeinde" or open-air people's assembly. On the last Sunday in April or the first Sunday in May, every citizen establishes what can be termed as direct contact with his government in a solemn ceremony by casting his vote for the executive officials on cantonal issues and legislative proposals. The "Landsgemeinde" dates back to the time of the formation of the old Confederation. The same system was practised in Schwyz and

Zug until 1848, in Uri until 1928/29 and in Appenzell Outer-Rhodes until 1997. It still persists in a large number of Grisons districts, but is restricted to the election of the "Landammann" (head of the relevant administrative district), court officials and representatives in the local parliament (Grand Council). On 1 January 2009, the Swiss Confederation had 2'636 communes. Their number is steadily declining, however, as every year some of the smallest communes merge. The Swiss communes represent small republics, many of which, like the Cantons, enjoy a high degree of autonomy. Swiss

The consolidated Federation found expression architecturally in the Federal Palace (1852–1902). The long complex of buildings comprises three main sections which were constructed successively, namely Parliament Building West (1852–1857), Parliament Building East (1888–1902) and the central link featuring a dome between the two sections, which also houses the parliamentary chambers. The Federal Palace enjoys a prominent position on the Aare peninsula. During the summer drifting along on the river is a popular pastime not only for people working in the federal administration, but also for everyone living and working in the city.

democracy can be seen in its most direct form at communal level. By participating in the local Commune Assembly – which is increasingly giving way to elected communal parliaments in the more populous communes – and by voting, the citizens themselves elect their communal or municipal authorities and run their own affairs. The responsibilities of the communes are wide-ranging: administration of public property, such as forests, water, gas and electricity supply; bridges, roads and administrative buildings; schools; the police, fire service, health departments and civil defence, etc.; also social, cultural and military concerns and the implementation of certain economic measures imposed in the event of war or disasters.

The administrative autonomy of the communes and the Cantons allows every citizen to play an active part in the democratic aspect of public life and in local affairs. The communes also collect direct and indirect taxation.

The wide diversity of Switzerland's communes reflects the country's pronounced regional differences and long history. The differences are discernible mostly in local area and size of population, but also show up in the nature of the commune: there are rural areas, largely industrial and commercial towns and, finally, settlements with a big-city character. A commune can cover a larger area than a small Canton, while certain "micro-communes" are smaller than an urban district.

Parliament

At national level, legislative power is vested in the Federal Assembly which is composed of two Chambers: the National Council representing the people, and the Council of States representing the Cantons. Two hundred members are elected to the National Council – each Canton and half-Canton has at least one member; election is based on proportional representation, except in Cantons which have only one representative, in which case the majority election system is used. In the Council of States, the 20 Cantons are each represented by two delegates, while the six half-Cantons have one member each. Every federal law or decree has to be passed by both Chambers which usually meet at the same time but in separate rooms. Moreover, both Chambers act as a militia parliament, supervising the federal administration and the enforcement of justice.

The two Chambers come together at least once a year as the united Federal Assembly to elect the Federal Council (Government), its President and Vice-President, the Federal Chancellor (Chief of Staff of the Government), the Federal Court (in Lausanne and Lucerne), the Military Court of Appeal and, in times of crisis, a General in charge of the armed forces. Parliament controls the army and has the power of pardon.

According to the Federal Constitution, every member of either Chamber can propose a law or decree. Each member can use his right of initiative either as a motion or a postulate.

A motion is an independent request to the Federal Council to present a new law or decree; a motion can also give binding directives to the Federal Council on measures to be taken or propositions to be made. A motion accepted by one Chamber is not binding on the Federal Council until the other Chamber agrees to it. A postulate is an independent request by which the Federal Council is invited to examine whether a law or decree should be proposed, or binding instructions should be given for any other action, on any particular issue. In addition, there is the parliamentary initiative. Furthermore, any

The "Landsgemeinde" or open-air people's assembly is the most obvious expression of direct democracy: in Appenzell the men and women entitled to vote gather on the Landsgemeindeplatz on the last Sunday in April. They pass resolutions regarding important state matters, i.e. business of the Canton of Appenzell Inner Rhodes. In addition, they elect the Standeskommission (cantonal government) and the Landammann (government president). Thus, on this particular day, individual citizens have a rare opportunity, once a year, to become acquainted with the canton's and the federal government's problems and, at the same time, are reminded of the tradition which has been handed down.

However, state-of-the-art technology is also used for elections : from 2005, a number of pilot regions have been carrying out successful trials of E-Voting – voting via the internet or a mobile phone.

Council Member is entitled to present an oral or written interpellation or simply to ask in writing for information on any subject concerning affairs of state. In addition, there is a so-called "question time" twice per session in the National Council.
www.parliament.ch

The Federal Council

Executive authority is vested in the Federal Council, which is elected every four years by the Federal Parliament. It presides over the seven Federal Departments (Ministries), ensures that current laws are observed and drafts new legislation; it conducts foreign affairs and authorises the mobilisation of troops. The Federal Council operates by the collegiate system, with collective responsibility for decisions. The President of the Confederation, nominated in rotation for a one-year term, takes the chair at Federal Council meetings but otherwise has no special powers or privileges over the other Members and continues as Head of his own Department. The so-called "magic formula" has been in force since 1959, according to which the four main parties are

The Federal Council in 2009 (from left to right): Federal Councillor Ueli Maurer, Federal Councillor Micheline Calmy-Rey, Federal Councillor Moritz Leuenberger, Federal President Hans-Rudolf Merz, Federal Councillor Doris Leuthard (Vice-President), Federal Councillor Pascal Couchepin, Federal Councillor Eveline Widmer-Schlumpf and Federal Chancellor Corina Casanova.

represented on the Federal Council more or less proportionally. At present, the Radical Free Democratic Party (FDP) and the Social Democratic Party (SP) each have two seats, while the Christian Democratic Party (CVP), the Swiss People's Party (SVP) and the Conservative Democratic Party (BDP) – which was formed in 2008 by a splinter group from the Swiss People's Party – each have one seat in the government. The three largest Cantons, Zurich, Berne and Vaud, have regularly been represented by one Federal Councillor since 1848. In practice, the election of a Federal Councillor is the result of an extremely complex "political chemistry". A subtle and delicate balance has to be struck in terms of language, denominational, regional and political considerations, etc. and an acceptable compromise reached. The majority of Swiss people expect their politicians – and in particular Federal Councillors – to be discreet and efficient.

In 1984 a woman was elected Federal Councillor for the first time – Elisabeth Kopp from Zurich, a member of the Radical Free Democratic Party. Following Ruth Dreifuss, Ruth Metzler, Micheline Calmy-Rey and Doris Leuthard, Eveline Widmer-Schlumpf, who has been in office since 2008, became the sixth female minister to be elected to the Federal Government. In addition, the Swiss parliament elected the first female Federal Chancellor in 1999: Annemarie Huber-Hotz was formerly Secretary-General of the Federal Parliament. She was succeeded on 1 January 2008 by Federal Chancellor Corina Casanova, who had been Vice-Chancellor since 2005.

Federal Administration

Approximately 36'000 people work in the general federal administration. The Federal Administration departments include Foreign Affairs (FDFA), Defence/Civil Protection/Sports (DDPS), Finances (FDP), Justice and Police (FDJP), Economic Affairs (FDEA), Environment/Transport/Energy/Communications (DETEC) as well as Home Affairs (FDHA) which is responsible among other things for culture, education, health and social matters.

www.admin.ch

A quartet with a great deal of responsibility: Doris Leuthard, Head of the Federal Department of Economic Affairs (FDEA) and Vice-President, Micheline Calmy-Rey, Minister for Foreign Affairs (FDFA), Eveline Widmer-Schlumpf, Justice Minister (FDJP) and Corina Casanova, Federal Chancellor.

A view of the National Council room from the spectators' gallery. This is where the 200 national councillors sit. Since the introduction of voting and electoral rights for women in 1971, the proportion of women in the National Council and Council of States has steadily increased. In 2008, 57 of the 200 National Council seats and 10 of the 46 Council of State seats were occupied by women

The Federal Court

The highest judicial authority lies with the Federal Court based in Lausanne. As the court of last resort, the Federal Court lays down a de facto, definitive interpretation of the law as a guideline for the country as a whole. The Federal Court also acts as a State Tribunal in matters of conflict between individual Cantons, or between a Canton and the Confederation. Finally, the Federal Court serves an important function in upholding the constitutional rights of citizens against arbitrary measures taken by the authorities and the administration, though it does not protect them against wrong decisions by the legislature. The Federal Court of Insurance in Lucerne, an independent department of the Federal Court, is called upon to act on complaints and claims in matters of social security. In addition, there are two federal courts of first instance intended to take some of the burden from the supreme court: the Federal Criminal Court in Bellinzona started operation in 2004. It rules in the first instance on criminal cases which fall under the jurisdiction of the Confederation. These include, for example, major organised crime cases and economic crimes, money laundering and corruption. The Federal Administrative Court began its work in 2007 in Berne and will move to St Gallen in 2010. The main task of the Federal Administrative Court is to rule on public law disputes arising from the jurisdiction of the Federal Administration. **www.bger.ch** (Federal Court)

Semi-direct democracy

"It is an overwhelmingly difficult task to describe a nation; even more so when it doesn't exist", so said the writer C.-F. Ramuz in a text he wrote in 1937 whose severe attitude to the Swiss caused quite a stir. It is in fact, nigh on impossible to attribute obvious common denominators to the Swiss in 26 Cantons and half-Cantons. On the political scene, one rarely encounters great demonstrations, passionate debates or spectacular confrontations. The division of the country into 26 Cantons and half-Cantons to which great administrative and political authority is devolved, and the fact that each of them has its own parliament and government have resulted in the political life in Switzerland taking place mainly at the communal and cantonal levels, which lead an independent political existence. Federal affairs are, nevertheless, playing an increasingly important role. While there were only 94 plebiscites held between 1900 and 1950, there where no fewer than 324 between 1950 and 2000.

The number of initiatives put before the Federal Chancellery has also greatly increased since the fifties; between 1991 and 2000 there were 56. One paradoxical factor is that while the number of plebiscites held has increased, participation by voters has dropped. Until the fifties, the regular turnout was generally above 50%; this has considerably decreased and nowadays wavers between 33% and 50%. It is a similar story for votes taken at cantonal level where participation is generally even lower – often less than 30%.

Despite extensive discussion, the true reasons for this abstention are far from being clear. One fact, however, stands out: political intervention is becoming less and less the exclusive preserve of the parties. All over the country, people are forming citizens' committees, united over a particular issue and determined to act as pressure groups and make use of the referendum and right of initiative. **www.bk.admin.ch**

Some important plebiscites (extract)

2000 Sectorial agreements, called "Bilateral Agreements", between Switzerland and the European Union were approved.

2001 The "indebtedness brake", a mechanism to restrict federal indebtedness, was approved.

2002 Approval was given to an Abortion Act, which allows for the termination of a pregnancy without prosecution within the first twelve weeks. Approval was also given to the popular initiative for the accession of Switzerland to the United Nations (UN).

2003 The electorate approved an additional democratic right by means of a "general popular initiative". Now, once the signatures of 100'000 Swiss people have been collected, it is possible not only to initiate changes to the Constitution, but also to the law.

2004 A further extension of the motorways, especially the extension of the Gotthard Road Tunnel, was rejected. The maternity insurance was approved in the autumn. There were also votes in favour of a law to govern human embryonic stem cell research in Switzerland.

There is scarcely a country that allows its citizens so many rights to participate in decision-making as does Switzerland. Citizens are entitled to call for a change in the constitution or the law through an Initiative (100'000 signatures), and for a plebiscite on federal laws and federal decrees with a Referendum (50'000 signatures). The Federal Constitution expressly grants freedom of private ownership, trade and commerce, residence, religion and philosophy, press, associations, petition. Citizens action groups that lend greater force to a Referendum or Initiative are commonplace. The freedom to demonstrate is also anchored in the Federal Constitution (the picture shows a demonstration on the Federal Square in Berne).

2005 Switzerland's participation in the EU agreements of Schengen and Dublin was approved. It was also resolved that Switzerland would gradually extend the current EU agreement on free movement of persons to include the ten new EU member states. Furthermore, a new Partnership Act was adopted to enable same sex couples to legally secure their relationship. The popular initiative on genetic engineering was also adopted. The Swiss agriculture industry may not plant any plants or rear any animals which are genetically modified for the next five years. The proposal to make it easier for young second generation foreign people to obtain citizenship and to grant automatic citizenship to third generation children of foreign people was rejected.

2006 "Yes" to cooperation with the countries of Eastern-Europe and "Yes" to the federal law on family allowances.

2007 The people's initiative for a unified social health insurance scheme was rejected.

2008 Adoption of the federal law on the improvement of general tax conditions for entrepreneurial activity and investments.

Federal Government finances

Tax rates, government expenditure and level of indebtedness are important financial policy reference data for the assessment of location attractiveness and competitiveness. The Federal Government's expenditure rate in recent years has been around 11 per cent. The tax rate has been around 10 per cent and the level of indebtedness 28 per cent.

The recovery strategy for federal finances followed in recent years is showing some effect: in 2007, the Confederation achieved a surplus of 4 billion francs, with spending of just under 54 billion and income of a good 58 billion Swiss francs. The global financial crisis in 2008 is making it difficult to implement the planned positive budget for 2008. The prospects for the coming years are clouded by the emerging economic crisis and global signs of a recession.

www.efv.admin.ch (Federal Finance Administration)

Federal Finances for 2008

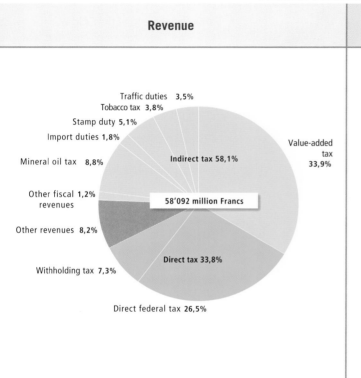

Revenue

58'092 million Francs

- Traffic duties 3,5%
- Tobacco tax 3,8%
- Stamp duty 5,1%
- Import duties 1,8%
- Mineral oil tax 8,8%
- Other fiscal revenues 1,2%
- Other revenues 8,2%
- Withholding tax 7,3%
- Direct federal tax 26,5%
- **Indirect tax 58,1%**
- Value-added tax 33,9%
- **Direct tax 33,8%**

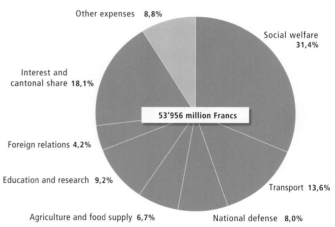

Expenditure

53'956 million Francs

- Other expenses 8,8%
- Social welfare 31,4%
- Interest and cantonal share 18,1%
- Foreign relations 4,2%
- Education and research 9,2%
- Agriculture and food supply 6,7%
- National defense 8,0%
- Transport 13,6%

Source: Swiss Financial Administration 2008

The Federal Department of Defence, Civil Protection and Sports has a wide variety of duties. It is part of the army's remit, amongst other things, to protect the population and its livelihood in the event of natural disasters. During the severe storms in 2005 more than 2'700 members of the forces were in action at times. During this period, they provided more than 30'000 days of service. Among other things, they maintained an airlift to the mountain village of Engelberg in Central Switzerland, which was cut off from its surroundings for days. In the Matte district of Berne the forces erected barricades made of sandbags against the Aare which had burst its banks (pictured).

National defence

Following the end of the Cold War the Swiss Army has been reformed and the age and number of its members reduced, but remains a militia army. In 2004, the current army was created in the course of the most significant reform in the history of the Swiss Army. It consists of just under 135'000 men and women. The Federal Constitution has allotted three duties to the army: preventing armed conflict, helping to maintain peace and defending the nation and its people. It supports the civil authorities in defending against serious internal security threats and managing other extraordinary situations.

Every year the Army contributes thousands of working days to public safety activities in avalanche areas, cases of flooding, caring for refugees and embassy protection. The Civil Defence becomes involved in repair work in the wake of storms, looking after the residents of residential homes, major sporting events or Swiss festivals.

Switzerland has also been involved in peace promotion with up to 220 Swisscoy volunteers in the Kosovo peace mission, these volunteers being armed for self-protection.

Since 1990 Switzerland has also been involved in military observation deployments. Observers are always unarmed. As military experts, they monitor compliance with ceasefire agreements and peace treaties. They are popularly known as "blue berets". There are more than 20 Swiss officers acting as UN military observers. They are currently deployed in the Middle East, Georgia, the Democratic Republic of Congo, in Nepal and Burundi.

A total of 6,5 million days of military service are performed each year. The Swiss Army is based on compulsory military service for all male citizens and the militia principle. Both are anchored in the Constitution.

Women may join the army as volunteers and all posts are open to them; in the Swiss Air Force, for example, there are female helicopter and jet pilots. In 2008, 1'050 women joined the army as volunteers.

At the age of 20 each conscript is called up for an 18 to 21-week basic course for new recruits. This is followed by six to seven three-week refresher courses. Total military service amounts to at least 260 days and should be completed by the age of 34. Up to 15 per cent of each annual intake of recruits can perform their entire training duty in one go as "Durchdiener" (recruits doing uninterrupted military service) and then remain in the Reserve Army for ten years. Officers serve for considerably longer and can be called up until they are 50. The Swiss Army is divided into brigades and battalions.

www.vbs.admin.ch

Swiss forces are also deployed abroad: in the Suva Reka area in Kosovo up to 220 Swiss soldiers and guards in the "Swisscoy" provide support for the international peacekeeping force in Kosovo (KFOR).

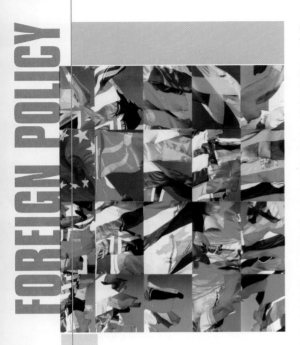

GROWTH THROUGH THE CENTURIES

Swiss foreign policy pursues five main goals, namely the peaceful coexistence of nations, respect for human rights and promotion of democracy, safeguarding the interests of the Swiss economy abroad, alleviation of need and poverty in the world, and preservation of natural resources. Switzerland has been a member of the United Nations since 2002. Switzerland concluded the Free Trade Agreement with the EU in 1972 and also numerous additional sectorial agreements, including the "Bilateral Agreements" I (1999) and II (2004). These strengthen Switzerland's position as a centre of economic activity, provide easier access to the European internal market and form the basis of cooperation with the EU in a series of other important political fields.

www.swissworld.org

The objectives of Swiss foreign policy

The main objectives of Swiss foreign policy are set out in the new Federal Constitution which has been in force since 1st January 2000. The Swiss Federal Council has defined its five priorities in the "Foreign Policy Report 2000 – Presence and Cooperation: Safeguarding Switzerland's Interests in an Integrating World" for the first decade of the third millennium.
www.eda.admin.ch
(Federal Department of Foreign Affairs)

Increase of pacific activities:

Switzerland wishes to make a substantial contribution to the prevention of violent conflicts. Particular priorities include the furtherance of democracy and the rule of law, the promotion of dialogue in the event of conflicts and reconstruction efforts. Switzerland wishes to contribute to an open discourse and increase respect, both nationally and internationally, for cultural diversity by means of an "intercultural dialogue".

Continuation of humanitarian policy:

Switzerland conducts its human rights policies in accordance with the principles of the universality and indivisibility of human rights. In continuation of its foreign policy tradition Switzerland wishes to pursue an independent humanitarian policy and increase its efforts to achieve respect for and promotion of human rights, democracy and the rule of law.

Safeguarding economic interests:

The government wishes to secure the best possible domestic conditions for the Swiss economy, and thus the preconditions for its success at international level. Thematic priorities are export promotion for SMEs (small and medium-sized enterprises), support through foreign policy for Switzerland's position as a centre of research and education, and multilateral and bilateral commitment to good general conditions worldwide. The promotion of Switzerland's position as an efficient and competitive financial centre and the safeguarding of its interests abroad are of particular importance.
www.seco.admin.ch
(State Secretariat for Economic Affairs)
www.osec.ch
(Business Network Switzerland)
www.economiesuisse.ch
(Umbrella association for the Swiss economy)

Increasing financial support and making the fight against poverty a central element of Swiss development aid:

Switzerland wishes to set the following priorities regarding its development cooperation activities: promotion of income and employment, "good governance", promotion of the private sector, sustainable use of natural resources, integration into world trade, debt relief, social equalisation, and preventing and overcoming crises. Switzerland wishes to provide public development cooperation funding amounting to 0,4% of Swiss GNP.
www.deza.admin.ch

Commitment to environmental policy:

In its international environmental policy Switzerland wishes to work for the further development and enforcement of legal instruments which create a strong international environmental system. Its most pressing concerns are to consolidate existing treaties, especially in the climate, biological diversity and chemicals fields, as well as to create international rules for the protection of forests and water. **www.umwelt-schweiz.ch**

Centre of worldwide cooperation: Nowhere in the world hosts as many international conferences and meetings as Geneva: more than 120'000 delegates travel to Geneva every year. 25 international organisations have their headquarters in Geneva, nine of which belong to the UN system. This makes Geneva the second most important seat of the UN after New York; (the picture shows the United Nations Palace of Nations) and, in addition, a central platform for Swiss foreign policy. The members of the diplomatic representations from more than 150 states and international officials, together with their dependants, number approximately 35'000.

In order to ensure resources are used as efficiently as possible, Switzerland is aiming to give its bilateral foreign policy a clearer geographical focus, giving greater attention in particular to South-eastern Europe and the Mediterranean. One of Switzerland's strengths is its extensive network of foreign agencies. Switzerland is present abroad with, all in all, almost one hundred embassies and as many consular agencies and coordination offices for development cooperation.

Neutrality

Switzerland's neutrality means that it has an obligation not to take part in any international armed conflicts. Switzerland's neutrality remains a significant factor in Swiss foreign and security policy as a peace-related and humanitarian instrument. As a neutral country, Switzerland cannot enter into any obligation to assist in the event of war, nor can it provide military support to any party to a conflict. However, its neutrality does not apply in the event of sanctions being imposed by the UN. Switzerland supports those sanctions decided on

The Swiss Confederation's international cooperation and humanitarian aid are important areas of Swiss foreign policy. The Swiss Agency for Development and Cooperation (SDC) in the Federal Department of Foreign Affairs is derived in particular from the Federal Law regarding International Development Cooperation and Humanitarian Aid of 1976 and from the Federal Resolution regarding Cooperation with the States of Eastern Europe of 1995.
In order to achieve the maximum possible effect, the SDC pursues the principle of sustainability in its long-term development work and helps people to help themselves, for example by supporting small businesses in Mali (left).

Numerous projects are in place in Eastern Europe and Central Asia where strengthening of civil society is an important aspect of the transition process. An example of this is to be found in Bosnia-Herzegovina where SDC's work includes the support of advanced training in the public health sector (right). Humanitarian aid, on the other hand, is offered anywhere in the world where crisis situations and emergencies occur. Key areas of the operations that are carried out both by partners as well as with experts from the Swiss Humanitarian Aid Unit (SHA), are prevention, rescue, survival assistance, reconstruction and advocacy, the legal representation of victims' interests.

by the UN and, in this context, can grant rights of transit. Also consistent with Switzerland's neutrality is its cooperation as regards training and armaments with foreign partners, as this does not denote any obligation to assist in the event of war. The same applies to its participation in the "Partnership for Peace" and its membership of international organisations such as the Organisation for Security and Cooperation in Europe (OSCE) and the Council of Europe.

Switzerland and the UN

On 10th September 2002 Switzerland was admitted by the General Assembly of the UN in New York as a full member of the United Nations Organisation after the Swiss people and the Cantons agreed to Switzerland joining the UN in a Referendum in March 2002.
www.uno.admin.ch
Since its accession in September 2002, Switzerland has established itself as a partner in the UN whose cooperation and support are acknowledged and sought. In practice, Switzerland benefits particularly

well from being perceived as an independent country with no "hidden agenda" and no strategic ulterior motives.

In accordance with its foreign policy priorities, Switzerland is particularly committed to the promotion of peace, human security, the fight against poverty, human rights, international humanitarian law, the rule of law and democracy, the protection of minorities, environmental protection and sustainable development. Particular emphasis is placed on the efforts to reform the UN and the strengthening of multilateralism. Switzerland is playing a very active role in facilitating the implementation of the reform plans decided on in principle by the heads of state and government in September 2005. In March 2006 the UN member states approved the establishment of a Human Rights Council which replaced the discredited Human Rights Commission. Established as a result of an initiative proposed by Switzerland, this new UN body therefore also heralds a success for Swiss diplomacy. Switzerland has made every effort to ensure that the Human Rights Council becomes a strong, effec-

tive and fair UN body to protect and to promote human rights. Following its successful candidacy, Switzerland can continue its commitment as one of the 47 members of the new Human Rights Council. The new council has its headquarters in Geneva.

Switzerland – EU: Bilateral Agreements I

The Bilateral Agreements I between Switzerland and the European Union (EU) have been in force since 1st June 2002. This important group of agreements is predominantly composed of traditional market access agreements and regulates the relationship between Switzerland and the EU in the following areas: research, public procurement, technical barriers to trade, agriculture, air transport, overland transport and free movement of persons. The Bilateral Agreements place the economic relationship between Switzerland and the EU on a solid footing. The EU is Switzerland's most important supplier and customer: a good 60% of Swiss exports go into the EU while approximately

Der richtige Weg für die Schweiz.

www.bilaterale.ch

Erfolgreiche Bilaterale

The vote of 8 February 2009 is a landmark decision regarding the continuation of the bilateral route. By voting 'Yes' the voters ratified the good contractual framework, on the proven basis of which cooperation can be continued with the EU by means of bilateral agreements. A 'No' to the freedom of movement would have been tantamount to a termination of the bilateral agreements

80% of Swiss imports come from the EU. The seven agreements of the Bilateral Agreements I are legally linked: If one were to be revoked, all of the other six would be rendered invalid. The life of all of the agreements is indirectly dependent on the agreement on the free movement of persons. In 2009 Switzerland or, in the event of a Referendum, the people must decide whether this agreement will be continued. The free movement of persons will be introduced gradually and in a controlled manner. Since 1st June 2004 the same treatment has applied to those Swiss working in EU states as to EU citizens. In addition, thanks to a protection clause of the contract which remains in force until 2014, Switzerland will be able to temporarily reintroduce quotas in the event of excessive immigration.

Initial experiences of the Bilateral Agreements I are positive, with economie-suisse, the umbrella organisation covering the Swiss economy, considering them "indispensable". As a result of the enlargement of the EU on the 1st May 2004, the bilateral agreements between Switzerland and the EU, with the excep-

tion of the freedom of movement, have been automatically extended to the new EU member states. These agreements will consequently gain even more importance. Separate transitional provisions have been negotiated for the extension of the agreement on the freedom of movement as regards the new EU states, for example for quotas until 2011. These regulations came into force on the 1st April 2006.

Switzerland – EU: Bilateral Agreements II

Nine additional bilateral agreements, the so-called "Bilateral Agreements II" were concluded with the EU in 2004, some of which were "left over" from the first bilateral negotiations: pensions, processed agricultural products, the environment, statistics, the media, as well as education/professional training/youth. In addition, both the EU and Switzerland have introduced new concerns in the areas of fighting fraud, interest taxation and cooperation in the field of police and asylum (Schengen/Dublin). The Bilateral Agreements II again cover important economic interests of the financial centre, the food industry and tourism and, at the same time, cooperation with the EU is being extended to further key policy areas such as internal security, asylum policy, the environment, culture and education.

The second bilateral round of agreements has come into force with a few exceptions. The existing agreements are now to be quickly and efficiently implemented. New areas of interest are being examined with a view to further negotiations. In addition, Switzerland wishes to make a contribution towards the ten new EU states and thereby show its support and solidarity in helping to reduce social and economic inequalities in the expanded EU. Finally, with its report on Europe, the Federal Council is creating a basis for debate on the further course of action in European politics. **www.europa.admin.ch**

Cooperation in other organisations

Since 1963 Switzerland has been a member of the Council of Europe which, above all, is active in the areas of human rights,

"The Human Rights and Alliance of Civilizations Room."
In March 2006 the UN General Assembly passed a resolution to create a Human Rights Council. Switzerland had previously fought strongly for such a council. The Human Rights Council has its headquarters in Geneva and is made up of a further 46 states, in addition to Switzerland. As the host state of the Human Rights Council, Switzerland has undertaken to offer the Council, the delegates of the states which take a seat on the Council, the representatives of non-governmental organisations and the Office of the High Commissioner for Human Rights optimum general conditions.

185 national organisations belong to the International Federation of the Red Cross and Red Crescent Organisations in Geneva, including the Swiss Red Cross (SRC) in Berne. The country's oldest and largest relief organisation has a federal structure modelled on the Swiss Confederation. The SRC provides disaster relief abroad and participates with other national Red Cross organisations in reconstruction and development projects. The picture shows food being distributed in Swaziland in southern Africa.
www.redcross.ch

legal harmonisation, culture and social problems. Cooperating closely with the neutral and non-aligned states, Switzerland took part in the Conference on Security and Cooperation in Europe (CSCE) which was established in 1975; this was renamed the Organisation for Security and Cooperation in Europe (OSCE) in 1994 and now numbers 55 Member States. In addition, Switzerland is a member of the OECD (Organisation for Economic Cooperation and Development), the forum of the western industrial states.

Development cooperation and humanitarian aid

Switzerland participates in international development cooperation, providing financial aid and technical cooperation, taking commercial and economic policy measures and supporting economic reforms through social programmes. The Swiss Agency for Development and Cooperation (SDC) in the Federal Department of Foreign Affairs is responsible for overall coordination. As well as the bilat-

eral approach, multilateral cooperation has become increasingly important.
www.deza.admin.ch
The SDC helps people to help themselves and helps to improve the living conditions of the poorest people in the world. Thus, bilateral development cooperation focuses on 17 key countries and seven special programmes. On the other hand, the Swiss Confederation's Humanitarian Aid works all over the world with the Swiss Humanitarian Aid Unit (SHA) in the event of a disaster or crisis. Important partners in the multilateral spectrum are the UN organisations, the World Bank, the International Monetary Fund and the International Committee of the Red Cross (ICRC).
The SDC is also engaged in Eastern Europe. Together with the SECO (State Secretariat for Economic Affairs) it is supporting the countries of South-eastern Europe and the CIS (particularly South Caucasus and Central Asia) during their transition to an open, democratic society and a social, sustainable market economy. Many projects take a more fundamental approach, complementing reforms at gov-

ernment level: democracy is therefore being stimulated from below by the establishment of community forums, the promotion of the media and the strengthening of civil society.

The International Committee of the Red Cross (ICRC) provides important humanitarian aid all over the world. Switzerland supports the ICRC both for its headquarters functions in Geneva as well as for its operational activities in the field. The ICRC provides assistance to crisis victims, promotes international humanitarian law, acts as a neutral intermediary and also ensures that the Geneva conventions are observed in armed conflicts. Its principle lays down that persons who are not or are no longer immediately involved in acts of war are to be treated with humanity at all times. The picture shows the International Red Cross and Red Crescent Museum at the headquarters of the ICRC in Geneva.
www.icrc.org

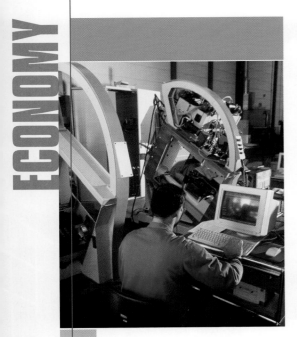

PLENTY OF IDEAS BUT FEW NATURAL RESOURCES

Industrial development in most countries started with the exploitation of natural resources such as iron and coal. This was not the case with Switzerland which has no such traditional supply of raw materials. Only hydroelectricity is plentiful. And human capital, i.e. numerous well-trained and innovative experts. Together, these two factors have resulted in the excellent reputation of Swiss industry, which manufactures products of the highest quality for demanding applications and world-famous brand products. As the home market is small, almost all of the products manufactured in Switzerland have to be sold abroad. This has become a characteristic feature of the economy, even if, as everywhere, the market is now dominated by the diverse service sector.

www.swissworld.org

The service industry helps to maintain the balance of trade

Two thirds of Switzerland is made up of forest, lakes, glaciers and rock. The agricultural land available is not sufficient to feed the population. In addition, each hour about one square metre of land is still disappearing under streets or buildings. And there are no mineral resources either.

And yet Switzerland has recorded stable economic growth for over 150 years. One secret of its success is its well-educated workforce, which favours the development of efficient industrial and service-sector companies. In many cases, industry concentrates on highly developed niche products. Internationally standardised mass-production goods constitute an exception. A large proportion of industrial products and also many services are exported.

For this reason, Switzerland – like other small industrialised countries – is dependent on open world markets. It has long been a contributor to the work of international economic organisations, whether the UN's specialised agencies or the World Trade Organisation (WTO). Since 2002 Switzerland has also been a full member of the United Nations (UN). Currently, well over half the active population work in the service sector. They account for two thirds of gross domestic product (GDP), the total value of goods and services produced within the domestic economy. Swiss banks and insurance companies are among the international leaders in this branch. The scenic advantages are additionally enjoyed in both summer and winter by many foreign visitors and make Switzerland a major country for tourism.

Foreign trade

Switzerland's economy relies on foreign trade to a large extent, both for imports and exports. Since time immemorial Swiss trade policy has therefore been based on the principles of a free market. For many years customs duty on industrial goods has been low, there are hardly any import quotas, with agricultural products constituting a controversial exception. Switzerland is one of the countries with the highest proportions of the gross domestic product being provided by foreign trade. Switzerland's most important trading partners are the industrialised countries, to which 77,9% of goods were exported and from which 88,1% of goods were imported in 2007. The EU is of particular importance to Switzerland (62,0% of exports, 79,5% of imports).

The balance of trade fluctuates between a deficit and a surplus, depending on the

Foreign trade, goods classified by intended purpose

Value in millions of francs	Imports 2007	2006	Exports 2007	2006
Raw materials, semifinished goods	52'091	43'608	45'161	40'574
Energy supplies	13'184	13'986	4'945	4'679
Capital goods	47'274	42'803	58'628	53'071
Consumer goods	71'029	65'013	88'799	79'151
Precious metals and precious stones	7'292	10'182	6'546	6'149
Works of art and antiques	2'346	1'556	2'173	1'592
Total	193'216	177'148	206'252	185'216

Source: Swiss Customs Administration

Development of Swiss foreign trade 2005-2007

(excl. precious metals and precious stones as well as works of art and antiques)

Year	Balance million CHF	Imports million CHF	Exports million CHF	Imports 1000 tonnes	Exports 1000 tonnes
2005	7'883,0	149'094,3	156'977,3	47'159	15'109
2006	12'064,5	165'410,3	177'474,8	49'943	16'494
2007	13'954,9	183'577,8	197'532,7	49'816	16'997

Source: Swiss Customs Administration

Overview of Switzerland's balance of payments in 2007 (billion CHF)

	Income	Expenditure	Balance
Goods	197,5	183,6	13,9
Tourism	14,6	12,3	2,3
Financial services	24,6	2,1	22,5
Work income	2,1	14,5	-12,4
Capital income	154,3	115,8	38,5
Current transfers			-11,3
Total	393,1	328,3	53,5

Source: Swiss National Bank

year. In recent years, however, Switzerland has constantly succeeded in achieving a trade balance surplus, achieving a record high of 13 billion francs in 2007. Since 2003, Switzerland's balance of payments on current account, which is made up of surplus revenue from freight traffic, services as well as labour and capital income, has been in the black to the tune of 55-70 billion francs each year.

www.seco.admin.ch
(State Secretariat for Economic Affairs)
www.statistik.admin.ch
(Swiss Federal Statistical Office)
www.zoll.admin.ch
(Swiss Customs Administration)
www.snb.ch (Swiss National Bank)

In 2007, direct investments by Swiss companies abroad (capital exports) amounted to approximately 57 billion francs. The amount of annual direct investments fluctuated noticeably, as they are governed to a great extent by acquisitions abroad. Conversely, foreign direct investments in Switzerland amounted to 46 billion francs. This corresponded to the highest value recorded to date in 2007, with acquisitions again being crucial here. Amounting to 43 billion the investments originated almost exclusively from the EU.

Many Swiss companies are now operating globally. Nestlé, the world's largest multinational producing foods – both for humans and animals – has grown from Henri Nestlé's factory producing infant food from milk powder. Only about 1,5% of the approximately 230'000 employees now work in Switzerland. The major pharmaceuticals, insurance and banking corporations also realise only a small proportion of their turnover in Switzerland. The same applies to many specialised mechanical engineering or service companies. Swiss Re outstrips all of the other reinsurance companies in the world – and therefore suffers more financially from devastating whirlwinds in the USA than from Swiss floods.

But, conversely, the Swiss also play their part in worldwide economic integration: the world-famous Chevrolet brand of street cruisers from Detroit (USA) goes back to Louis Chevrolet, a watchmaker's son from La Chaux-de-Fonds (Canton of Neuchâtel) who emigrated before the First World War. Brown Boveri, a successful company and a leader in technology in its field, merged as early as 1988 with the Swedish firm Asea to form an international entity ABB. The language of communication in the Group is English; production is located all around the world. Other companies, such as Swisscom, are outsourcing their software development to India, whilst the pharmaceuticals corporation Novartis – which was established in 1996 following the merger of the Basle companies Ciba-Geigy and Sandoz – is extending its research laboratory in the USA for vast sums of money.

The world is also interconnected, however, by the Internet and other telecommunications media. In this respect, Switzerland is firmly integrated. Broadband connections, mobile telephones and the Internet are used intensively in business as well as in the private sphere. The transformation of the economy appears to be increasingly rapid and all-encompassing. The "rules" of an increasingly global market, which can seldom be fathomed, create a sense of insecurity. "Globalisation" often arouses opposition in Switzerland as well, directed for instance at the World Trade Organisation (WTO) and the World Economic Forum (WEF) in Davos, the annual meeting of key decision-makers in business and politics. The right of society and politics to have a say in how the economy is run is being demanded. The objective is meant to be the "promotion of common welfare and sustainable development" for all people, as enshrined in Article 2 ("Purpose") of the Federal Constitution.

Growth and recession

Immediately after the Second World War Switzerland, which had been spared the war, entered a long phase of economic growth. Between 1960 and 1973, Swiss economic performance grew on average by more than 4% per year. Prosperity and living standards rose considerably.

This boom was based on intensive investment, rising employment among Swiss workers and a large number of foreign workers brought into the country. The public services were expanded considerably. At the same time, thanks to the strong rate of growth, an extremely high proportion of the total population who were able to earn a livelihood and almost no unemployment, it was possible to set up a solid social se-

Economic data for Switzerland

Average annual increase in Gross Domestic Product (GDP), for the time periods:

1948–1975: 3,7%   1975–1990: 2,0%   1990–1996: 0,2%   1996–2000: 2,4%   2001–2005: 1,3%

Year	GDP[1] at 2005 prices (billion Fr.)	GDP growth rate[2] in %	Inflation[3] in %	Unemployment rate[4] in %
2003	440'667	-0,2	0,6	4,1
2004	451'828	2,5	0,8	4,0
2005	463'139	2,5	1,2	3,8
2006 [5]	478'809 [5]	3,4 [5]	1,1	3,3
2007 [5]	494'734 [5]	3,3 [5]	0,7	2,8
2008 [6]	503'782 [6]	1,8 [6]	2,4	3,0
2009 [6]	501'218 [7]	-0,5 [7]	0,7 [7]	3,5 [7]

Sources: Economic Reserarch Office, Fed. Institute of Technology, Zurich
[1] Gross domestic product corresponds to the value of goods manufactured on Swiss soil
[2] According to the national index of consumer prices
[3] Unemployed people registered with an employment office as a percentage of the working population
[4] Proportion of registered unemployed at year's end out of total working population
[5] GDP: provisional forecast FOS, [6] GDP: Estimation/forecast KOF [7] Forecast KOF

curity system, particularly for the elderly, without making any apparent sacrifices. The first serious slump of this "economic miracle", as of 1974, recalled to mind the limits to growth. Called the "Energy Crisis", the dip in growth showed that the high growth rate was due, first and foremost, to careless consumption of energy and wasteful use of natural resources. At the same time, there was a growing anti-immigrant movement.

Some fundamental changes were introduced. The influx of foreign workers was staunched and environmental protection became the priority political aim. Between 1974 and 1990 the average rate of growth halved to approximately 2%. But during this period Switzerland managed to maintain its high standard of living and even to further improve it for many people. At the end of the '80s the labour market had practically run dry once more, large numbers of foreign workers were again coming into the country and the property prices reached undreamt-of heights.

From 1990 onwards the motor of the economy started to misfire. Measured in terms of real growth, Switzerland slid to a clear position at the bottom of the scale in comparison with other industrial countries. Unemployment rose abruptly and by the end of 1996 was above the 5% mark. A considerable slump in real estate prices brought many banks and dealers to financial ruin. Public authorities closed the year with a deficit. Savings or at least curbed growth in expenditure became a widespread political objective. This only served to increase stagnation, however. The value of the Swiss franc rose dramatically, but this led to a worsening of the Swiss economy which became less competitive. Later, investment was only driven by the economic recovery and the euphoria associated with information technology and telecommunications in Switzerland until the turn of the millennium. At the same time, the share prices of the companies involved rose to dizzying heights.

Both bubbles burst in 2001. Instead of achieving gains, many investors had to write off billions of francs of losses. Insurance companies and pension funds were also affected. There was a risk of gaps in old-age provisions. In order to relieve the burden and to do justice to the increasing life expectancy, the guaranteed interest for old-age provisions was reduced from 4 to 2,25% in 2003. For the insured this means that their capital for their old age is increasing less than hoped. The Federal Council reduced the conversion rate at the same time. This percentage will be used to convert the capital saved to the old-age pension. Since then, the Swiss economy had been growing again until 2008 when the U.S. real estate crisis depressed the entire global economy, wiping billions off the value of share capital in Switzerland as well. Even the banking centre of Switzerland has been affected to an unprecedented extent. The repercussions of this crisis will shape the country in the coming years.

www.vorsorgeforum.ch
www.umwelt-schweiz.ch
www.swissre.com
www.travailsuisse.ch
(employees' umbrella organisation)

State and economy in partnership

The Swiss economy is based on the principle of free enterprise. Freedom in trade and industry is guaranteed by a constitutional article of 1874. Since that time, constitutional articles concerning the economy dating from 1947 and later have slightly tempered this freedom. State intervention is permitted if it can be justified in the interests of the country as a whole. For example, the Federal Council adopted dirigiste measures on a number of occasions and proclaimed a kind of "state of emergency" (prices and wages control, restriction of public building activities, etc.). The influence of associations and industry organisations has also increased. Experts from the business sector contribute to many committees, where laws and decrees are drafted, in the political "militia system" of Switzerland – and businesses are then frequently entrusted with the practical implementation of the regulations. In many issues Switzerland also relies on self-regulation of the relevant industries. Like the holes in a good-quality Swiss cheese, there are exceptions to the principle of free trade. For example,

many protectionist measures apply to agriculture, and also the importation of cars, brand-name articles or medicines and others, where numerous restrictions and exceptions still apply. Over two thirds of Swiss foreign trade is conducted with European countries, particularly with Germany and the other neighbouring countries in the European Union (EU). In 1992, a majority of voters rejected Swiss membership of the European Economic Area (EEA). Since then bilateral agreements have been concluded on two occasions (cf. the sub-section "Switzerland-EU" in the section "Foreign Policy"). They forge close links between Switzerland and the Economic Area with its 27 states and approximately 500 million people.
www.europa.admin.ch

Efficient social legislation

Soon after industrialisation began, the poor living conditions of the working population induced the State to concern itself with social questions. In 1877 the Federal Factories Act, which among other things set limits on the employment of children, and from 1890 onwards the Federal Acts concerning medical and accident insurance were passed. Mention should also be made of the constitutional article of June 1981 which basically guarantees equal salaries for men and women doing the same job. In reality, however, the salaries for women doing the same job are still 10 to 20% lower.

A central element of the social security system is the "AHV" – Old Age and Survivors' Insurance – introduced in 1948. In June 1972 the so-called triple-pillar pension scheme was anchored in the Federal Constitution: the first "pillar" is a compulsory national old age and surviving dependants' pension scheme (AHV), intended to cover basic needs, and the disability pension (IV). The second "pillar" consists of employers' staff pension schemes which have also been compulsory since 1985. Employers must pay at least half of the contributions. These two "pillars" are intended to ensure that pensioners can enjoy the same standard of living as they had before retiring. The third pillar, aimed at ensuring a sufficiently financially cushioned old age, is in fact a form of saving that benefits from tax relief (accounts, stocks, life insurance). Thanks to

The proportion of senior citizens in the total population is steadily growing. The so-called triple-pillar scheme for old-age provision is anchored in the Federal Constitution. However, the burden of the first pillar (Old Age and Survivors' Insurance) is falling to fewer and fewer contribution payers. The system, which depends on the younger generation to provide the pensions of the elderly, is threatening to collapse shortly unless a different financing option can be found.

Unemployment insurance			
Year	Number of unemployed	Expenditure in million Fr.	Revenue in million Fr.
1995	153'316	5'422	5'670
1996	168'630	6'453	5'962
1997	188'304	8'445	6'129
1998	139'660	6'566	5'928
1999	100'000	5'326	6'403
2000	71'987	3'917	6'673
2001	67'197	3'599	6'673
2002	100'504	5'200	7'200
2003	145'687	6'400	5'700
2004	153'091	7'540	5'268
2005	148'537	7'069	5'201
2006	131'532	6'300	5'200
2007	109'189	5'360	5'390

Source: State Secretariat for Economic Affairs

this triple-pillar system poverty in old age has now become rare.

A problem to which no adequate solution has yet been found, however, is economic support for families with low or average incomes. Maternity insurance was only approved in autumn 2004 after several referendums. A lack of childcare facilities for the children of working parents and concessions for families for taxes and medical costs are causing problems.
www.bsv.admin.ch
(Federal Office for Social Security)

Peaceful labour relations

Switzerland is among the countries which have the longest working hours, amounting to a good 1'800 hours per person per year. Since the climate in the working environment has got tougher, some workers have started to strike in Switzerland again. However, this is not calling into question the first "peace agreement" which was signed between trade unions and employers in the engineering industry in 1937. In most collective agreements (GAV), the signatories undertake not to use strike or lockout tactics respectively in the case of conflict and, if no agreement is reached, to call on the services of an arbitration board. Today, almost 600 collective agreements exist which cover around a third of all workers employed in the private sector. **www.statistik.admin.ch**

Small and medium-sized enterprises: backbone of the economy

The Swiss economy is based primarily on small, and very small, companies. This is often overlooked, because media headlines are generally dominated by the major cor-

porations, the high salaries of managers or the fluctuations in the price of their shares on the stock exchanges. However, in terms of quantity and number of jobs, the small and medium-sized companies (SME) dominate the economic reality of Switzerland. And very small companies, with fewer than ten employees, have been growing in particular during the last few years. Most activities in the service sector are conducted by small companies. On the other hand, in many cases, size brings economies of scale in industry and, to some extent, also in trade. In the 2001 census of companies, 97,9% of the 317'700 companies had fewer than 50 employees, and therefore counted as small or very small companies. The over 300'000 firms represent considerable potential in terms of entrepreneurial initiative – even if some of them were established more or less involuntarily, in the face of impending unemployment. In 2001, this size of company employed some 1,53 million people. This represented 47% of all those employed in the market economy, i.e. not counting state-sector employees. In terms of employment, the few major corporations have played a more substan-

tial role over the last few years. 1064 companies numbering 250 and more employees have provided employment for 1,06 million people, a third of all employees.
www.osec.ch (Business Network Switzerland)
www.seco.admin.ch, www.kmu.admin.ch

The chemical and pharmaceuticals industry

The Swiss chemical and pharmaceuticals industry had its roots in the silk and textile industry at home. Today, it is primarily based in the Basle area. What began with the production of dyes is now a world-leading chemical industry, especially in pharmaceuticals. For many years the industry was almost level with the engineering industry in terms of the proportion of products exported. However, since 2001, it has pulled away from it and now produces more than a third of all Swiss exports. However, the chemical industry was also the first industry to set up foreign subsidiaries and to go into international production.

A major surprise came in 1996 when Ciba-Geigy, which was already the product of the fusion of two Basle companies, merged with Sandoz to form Novartis, ensuring that one of the world's largest pharmaceuticals companies remained in Swiss hands. The success of the Swiss chemical and pharmaceuticals industry, which generates almost all its turnover outside Switzerland, is based on the enormous sums continually invested in research into new active substances and the development of new products. Almost 20'000 people are engaged in research and development throughout the world, swallowing several billion francs each year. By the time one new product reaches the market between 8'000 and 10'000 active substances have been tested, which can take anything from ten to twelve years. The Swiss dye industry is also one of the largest in the world and supplies high-quality products for dying and printing textiles, for the leather and paper industry, lacquers and varnishes, ink for the printing industry and dyes for the construction sector. Geneva is a centre for perfume and the production of food flavourings. The Swiss agro-chemical industry has achieved a high position worldwide mainly thanks to its plant protection products.
www.sgci.ch (Swiss Society of Chemical Industries)

Specialist know-how is essential for a functioning economy. An important part of this is a broad basic training in team and communication skills - not just in the machinery, electrical and metal industries. The picture shows electrical engineering apprentices in the Wifag machinery factory.

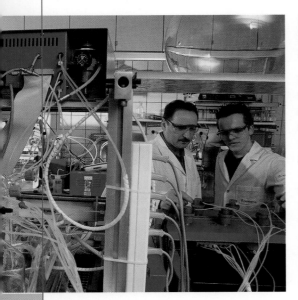

Industry invests well over 8 billion francs annually in research and development in Switzerland, and almost twice as much is spent on works in foreign laboratories. The chemical and pharmaceutical industry is responsible for more than thirty per cent of Swiss spending, with over forty per cent attributable to the machinery, electrical and metal industries.

Industry and the trades: The engineering, electrical and metal industries

The engineering, electrical and metal industries number more than 300'000 employees, more than half the number of employees of the processing industry. Swiss products range from the microscopic to the gigantic. The engineering industry is particularly renowned: Swiss machines can be found all over the world, rolling metal, spinning, weaving, milling, grinding, drilling, turning, milling grain, measuring, regulating, monitoring, controlling, switching, rolling, producing energy, pumping and reaping. There are many "unknown world champions" among small and medium-sized companies, which are world leaders in their specialist fields.

The Swiss engineering industry was originally created to meet the needs of the country's textile sector. The passage from manual labour to mechanised production in spinning and weaving mills dictated that the machine industry sector grew up in the areas where the mills were. At the end of the 18th century the Swiss wanted to outdo England which was the leading industrial nation in the textile industry. In addition, the British jealously guarded their machines and skilled labour. Today, the small country of Switzerland is well ahead, compared with all of the countries, from the point of view of exports of machinery and plant. Swiss companies rank highly in several markets, with the most competitive being the manufacturers of machinery for the paper industry, the machine-tool branch and the manufacturers of textile and printing machinery.

The Swiss engineering industry made a virtue out of necessity, namely its lack of raw materials, by creating the "Swiss Made" label famed for its high-precision quality production. Other major factors which boosted the machine-tool industry included the development of railways and steam-ships and the birth of the hydroelectric power industry at the end of the 19th century. In this field Swiss industry really made its mark with some 80 "firsts" including the turbo-generator (1898), the electric rack railway (Mont Salève near Geneva, 1890), the pump turbine (1930) and the gas-turbine power station (1978).

www.swissmem.ch

The watch industry

In the conquest of space or major sporting events, where time has to be measured to the millisecond, Swiss watches and chronometers will regularly be found at the forefront. The impeccable reputation of Swiss products in this sector has been founded on a high degree of inventiveness and a long-standing sense of high-quality workmanship.

At the end of the 16th century the Huguenot refugees brought with them the necessary technical expertise. Geneva was the home of the first guild of watchmakers at the beginning of the 17th century and the industry finally extended right along the Jura chain from Geneva to Schaffhausen. 1845 saw the arrival of the first machines capable of producing identical parts, thus creating the concept of mass production and turning craftsmanship into industry in one fell swoop. Thanks to mechanisation, the Swiss left their competitors behind, and for more than a century dominated the world market. Approximately 600 companies now employ 40'000 people. In 2007, the industry produced approximately 25,9 million finished

Economic sectors

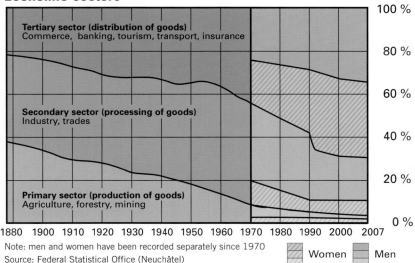

Note: men and women have been recorded separately since 1970
Source: Federal Statistical Office (Neuchâtel)

Women   Men

watches. Mechanical watches made up CHF 10 billion of the total value of the watches exported (CHF 16 billion). In terms of the value of the watches, Switzerland is therefore the largest watch exporter in the world. High-quality and expensive "Swiss Made" branded products sell exceptionally well thanks to the high quality of the products and the continuous improvements to the

components, as well as after-sales service. Almost all the major pioneering developments in watchmaking have come from Switzerland, which has become a synonym for timing. As early as 1921 the Swiss Laboratory of Horological Research was set up, followed by the Centre for Electronic Horology in 1962 and the Swiss Centre for Electronics and Microtechnology SA, in Neuchâ-

Economic structure by Canton

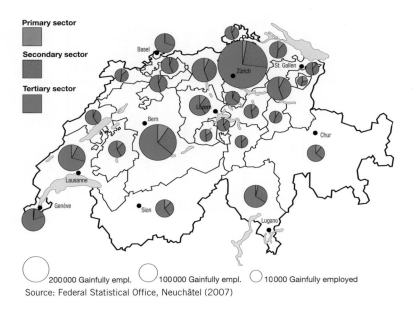

Primary sector

Secondary sector

Tertiary sector

200 000 Gainfully empl.   100 000 Gainfully empl.   10 000 Gainfully employed

Source: Federal Statistical Office, Neuchâtel (2007)

tel, in 1983. The latter concentrated on research into the possibilities of miniaturisation (microelectronics) and, in addition, in 1967 it produced the world's first quartz watch. Another important element is the world's only body certifying chronometers – the highly accurate timekeepers used especially in sport.

The Swiss watch industry continued to develop the quartz watch: numerical display using liquid crystal or electrochromic display, high-frequency quartz, and combined analogue and digital display. A recent addition is the thinnest watch in the world, boasting a "thickness" of just 0,98 mm. Despite all these pioneering achievements, Japanese and other Asian manufacturers managed to outdistance Switzerland with their cheap quartz watches. Along with the recession that hit the country's economy in the mid '70s this upheaval brought the whole Swiss watch industry to the brink of ruin. The number of jobs shrank dramatically. A quartz watch is in fact made up of far fewer components than a mechanical watch, and assembly is often automated. The turning point came only when the two largest watchmaking groups, which had fallen into financial difficulties, merged in 1983 to form what is now the Swatch Group. Swatch, a plastic watch which has become a fashion accessory and cult object thanks to ingenious advertising efforts, brought the industry high-volume sales again. For a few years now mechanical watches, which have no battery, have enjoyed a comeback. Watches in the top price ranges, in particular, are often fitted with a mechanical movement and their sales are very little affected by fluctuations in the economy. Here, and even more markedly so with richly-jewelled prestige watches which have a wide array of functions and can cost up to several million francs, the Swiss manufacturers supply almost the entire world market. **www.fhs.ch** (Association of the Swiss Watch Industry)

Agriculture

In a highly developed economy based on the division of labour, agriculture is closely connected to other sectors of the economy and to foreign countries. On the one hand, it uses many upstream services and products. On the other hand, agriculture supplies the market, whether it is the Saturday market in front of the Federal Parliament Building in Berne or the many processing plants. There are also close relationships, for instance, in the areas of training, basic research, applied research, consultancy and the supply of information. The agricultural sector's share of the Gross Domestic

Product (GDP) and of the number of persons in employment has been decreasing sharply for decades. This development and far-reaching structural changes are typical of virtually all modern economies (see table on page 67).

These proportions only inadequately reflect the real importance of agriculture: it uses and maintains approximately half of the entire territory of Switzerland and has had a marked effect on the landscape. Old cultivated areas are retained, natural habitats are preserved and decentralised settlement is increased. For Switzerland, as a destination for hikers and holidaymakers, the mountain landscape with its traditional alpine and summering regions is particu-

larly important. Farmers still characterise the economic, social and cultural life of the countryside as well. The majority of farms are family businesses, with agricultural policy being geared towards them. More often than not the farmers cultivate the land, the source of their workforce is the family, farms are merged, the farmers own the land they work and they live on the farm. **www.blw.admin.ch** (Federal Office for Agriculture)

Production and degree of self-sufficiency

Over the past 40 years yields have risen considerably thanks to the widespread

Use of land – total area: 41'284 km^2 (100%)

Type of use	km^2	%	Type of use	km^2	%
Pastures, arable land	9'264	22,4	No vegetation	6'156	14,9
Orchards, vines, Market gardening	610	1,5	Unprod. vegetation	2'631	6,4
Alpine pastures	5'378	13,0	Lakes and rivers	1'740	4,2
Agriculturally productive	**15'252**	**36,9**	**Unproductive**	**10'527**	**25,5**
Forest	11'021	26,7	Built-up areas	1'898	4,6
Bush, woods	1'690	4,1	Roads and railways	893	2,2
Total productive area	**27'963**	**67,7**	**Total unprod. area**	**13'318**	**32,3**

Source: Federal Statistical Office, Neuchâtel (2004)

Development of agricultural production in 1000 tonnes

Products	1955	1975	1995	1999	2000	2005	2007
Milk, total	2'825	3'396	3'930	3'852	3'871	3'933	4'008
Cheese	60,3	104	132	134	167	168	176
Butter	26,2	34,5	47,2	37,2	36,9	39,8	36,3
Meat	170,4	402,7	446	423,9	407,6	433	459
Eggs (per million)	535	720	592	647	652	630	631
Apples	280	435	199	229	375	213	277
Pears	310	192	124	78	117	64	84
Cherries	61	49	25	15	19	10	10
Plums	31	44	10	9	8	6	10
Wheat	321,9	341,3	618,1	489,4	561,2	521,4	535,6
Rye	28,6	24,4	42,1	18,3	22,4	9,4	10,1
Barley	63,3	172,3	303,4	250,7	274,1	231,2	210,9
Oats	59,2	44,6	44,1	27,8	26,3	15,3	10,1
Kernel maize	111	216	225	192,3	212,4	198,9	180,9
Potatoes	934,7	907,7	568,8	484	600,6	485	490
Sugar beet	209,9	479,4	824	1'187	1'410	1'409	1'573
Rape	8,7	32	45,2	38,4	39,1	56	56,5
Tobacco	2,3	1,6	1,6	1,5	1,6	1,2	1
Vegetables	285	258	390	301	310	313	313
Red wine (1000 hl)	194	332	530	591	606	522	528
White wine (1000 hl)	607	497	652	718	670	479	512

Sources: Federal Statistical Office, Neuchâtel (2007), Swiss Farmers' Union (2007).

application of technology, chemicals and agricultural science as well as improved organisation. Intensive farming has led to higher productivity per square kilometre and per animal, as well as per worker. Agricultural production almost doubled during this period – although energy consumption also rose sharply. The value of agricultural production (final output) is approximately CHF 10 billion. Thanks to favourable production conditions (climate, soils, topography, altitude, etc.) half of this amount was generated by plants and plant products as well as livestock. More than 80% of the agricultural surface area grows fodder for a good 1,5 million cattle (in particular for milk production) and just under 1,5 million pigs as well as approximately half a million sheep and goats. Over the past few decades the degree of self-sufficiency in Switzerland has risen thanks to developments in production techniques, on the one hand, and a slower growth in demand, on the other. Depending on the year's harvest, food produced within the country covers around 60% of the demand.

Development of the structure of agriculture			
	1985	2007	Change in %
No. of farms (excl. the smallest)	98'759	61'764	-37,5%
No. in mountain areas (excl. the Alps foothills)	41'600	25'324	-39,1%
No. in valleys	57'159	36'440	-36,3%
Main source of income	68'400	45'034	-34,2%
Size (area in hectares farmed, per full-time farm)	10,8	20,9	93,5%
No. of people employed in agriculture (full-time jobs)	300'500	77'846	-74%
No. of animals (in 1000s)			
Beef cattle	1'933	1'572	-18,7%
Pigs	2'191	1'573	-28,2%
Sheep	355	443	24,9%
Goats	79	79	+/-0%
Poultry	6'082	8'101	33,2%
Horses, donkeys, etc.	46	58	25,4%
Bee colonies	247	34,1*	-86,2%*
Equipment (piece)			
Tractors	105'300	107'000*	1,6%*
Farms with milking facilities	55'200	45'900*	-16,8%*

Source: Federal Statistical Officed, Neuchâtel * last information 2004

Agricultural policy: comprehensive reforms

With its seventh Agricultural Report, which was published in 1992, the Federal Council launched a comprehensive agricultural reform programme leading to radical changes in the agricultural sector at home and abroad. Key words include globalisation, deregulation and abolition of subsidies. The first step in implementing this programme was to introduce direct payments not based on products. This led, firstly, as stipulated in the World Trade Organisation's (WTO) agreements, to the separation of price and income policies. Secondly, other services provided by agriculture could be remunerated. Then, in 1996, an article on agriculture

Region	Area of forest in ha	Prop. of region forested in %	Private forest in %	Communal forest in %	Wood production in million m³
Jura	225'474	47,3	22,2	77,8	1,14
Mittelland	230'183	23,4	43,3	56,7	2,48
Foothills of the Alps	233'315	36,1	49,6	50,4	1,35
Alps	383'953	23,0	14,7	85,3	0,65
Southern side of Alps	171'756	48,4	18,8	81,2	0,92
Switzerland	**1'244'681**	**30,1**	**28,4**	**71,6**	**5,70**

Source: Yearbook "Forest and Wood 2007"

Avalanches often start at between 1'800 and 2'300 m above sea level, if the higher tracts of mountain forest have been destroyed. Various types of protective measures have been installed to prevent avalanches as well as to enable the forests to regenerate.

was added to the Federal Constitution and a totally revised law on agriculture came into force in 1999.

The measures which the Federal Council would like to implement with its "2011 Agricultural Policy" package, are being fiercely disputed. The core element of the 2011 Agricultural Policy is the considerable reduction of funds used to support prices and their transfer into direct payments. Export subsidies will be completely abolished and the funds for supporting the internal market will be more than halved. In addition, the tariffs for feedstuffs will be reduced. Careful treatment of land and animals is widespread, with more than 10% of all concerns being farmed

in accordance with strict organic guidelines. The proportion of organic food production can even be as much as 50% in the mountainous farming areas. Each year, agriculture and food cost the Federal Government almost 4 billion Swiss francs, some 7% of total expenditure. Direct payments to the farmers' families account for two thirds of this amount. **www.sbv-usp.ch**

Forestry

Forests are the natural habitat of many species of animal and plant life. For centuries, it has also supplied wood as a renewable source of raw materials and energy. The forest is of great importance as protection against avalanches, floods, erosion, mudflows and rock fall. The protective legislation culminated in the Federal Forests Act of 1876. Woodland clearance is prohibited. In cases where exceptional permission is granted the same area must be reforested in the vicinity.

The federal and cantonal authorities support economic use, forest management, care and protection as well as structural measures and the creation of forest tracks, also the training of forestry engineers and research. As a consequence of forest decline due to bark beetles and acid rain as well as Hurricanes Vivian and Lothar, the latter has acquired additional importance. Natural forest management involves increasingly relying on the regeneration of nature instead of reforestation by means of planting new trees. Thanks to these efforts and because much of the pasture in the mountain area is being abandoned, especially in Ticino, the forested area is increasing again – having increased by approximately 15% since 1965 alone. 1,27 million hectares or approximately 31% of Switzerland is forested. 9,5 million cubic metres of new timber grows each year, the entire timber supply of all living and dead trees in the Swiss forest was 420 million cubic metres in the 2007 Swiss National Forest Inventory. Of this approximately 90% is felled throughout Switzerland. This means that Swiss forests are maturing and becoming more abundantly stocked. In recent years, the proportion of near-natural forests and the ecological diversity in the forest have increased. Forestry employs around 75'000 people, mainly in rural areas.

Swiss manufacturers are also renowned for top-class quality in the textile industry. Many people wear sports clothes made of high-tech textiles with special characteristics. Mostly, models are only able to present selected Haute Couture at Parisian fashion shows: a "royal" creation of the Spring/Summer 2006 collection from Christian Lacroix (pictured).

Major hydroelectric plants

High head reservoirs	Canton	Total drop in metres	Active storage cap. million m³	Mean energy capability in million kWh
Grande Dixence	VS	1,882	400	2,100
Oberhasli	BE	1,638	196	1,587[1]
Hinterrhein	GR	1,264	215	1,482[2]
Maggia	TI	2,117	137	1,387[1]
Engadiner KW	GR	674	170	1,330
Mauvoisin	VS	1,866	205	1,000
Emosson/SBB	VS	1,478	238	947[3]
Blenio	TI	1,418	92	933
Cleuson-Dixence	VS	1,883[4]	–	155

[1] without pumped storage   [2] Swiss share = 1'380 million kWh
[3] Swiss share = 650 million kWh   [4] Highest single drop in the world

Source: Swiss Electricity Association (VSE)

Biggest Dams

Grande Dixence	285 m tallest gravity dam in the world
Mauvoisin	250 m second highest arch dam in use in Europe
Verzasca	220 m arch dam
Luzzone (Blenio)	223 m arch dam

Greatest cubic capacity:

Grande Dixence	5,96 million m³ concrete	
Mauvoisin	2,10 million m³ concrete	
Mattmark	10,50 million m³ earth	Height: 120 m
Göscheneralp	9,35 million m³ rockfill	Height: 155 m

Largest reservoirs:

Sihlsee	Area: 10,90 km²	Active storage capacity 92 million m³
Lac des Dix	Area: 4,03 km²	Active storage capacity 400 million m³

Source: Swiss Electricity Association (VSE)

The textile and clothing industry – small is beautiful!

The Swiss textile and clothing industry is admittedly very small by international standards, but is nonetheless an important export industry. Production levels are high and it is a very innovative and creative sector, famed for its high quality, variety and constant flow of new specialities. Only in this way can the industry make up for the disadvantages caused by its location (high salary costs, hard currency). Before industrialisation the textile industry was centred around Zurich (silk, 13th-15th century), Fribourg (weaving, 13th-15th century) and St. Gall (linen and later cotton). The original cottage-industry character was carried over into the largely decentralised textile industry in north-eastern Switzerland. The clothing industry is centred in Ticino. The Swiss textile industry's top fashion fabrics and embroidery still enjoy a high reputation among international haute couture designers. Elegant dreams made out of Swiss fabrics are in demand all over the world. Clothing fabrics represent almost half of production, furnishing fabrics around 30% and

technical materials approximately 30%. Approximately 90% of production is exported. Like the other export industries, the textile and clothing sector depends on open markets. In Europe duty-free access to markets is ensured by a free-trade agreement with the EU and a pan-European agreement with Eastern Europe which came into force in 1997. It would also be desirable to include the North African countries. High customs and import barriers frequently impede exports to other countries, in particular the important emerging states.
www.tvs.ch (Swiss Textiles Association)
www.economiesuisse.ch (Umbrella organisation for the Swiss economy)

The search for an energy policy

The basis of healthy economic development is an energy supply that is ensured in the long term. Swiss energy originates largely from other countries. Since 1990, the Federal Constitution has included an article devoted to energy. It calls for an economical and environmentally acceptable energy supply and the economical and efficient use of energy and, in particular, of domestic and

Final energy consumption in TJ

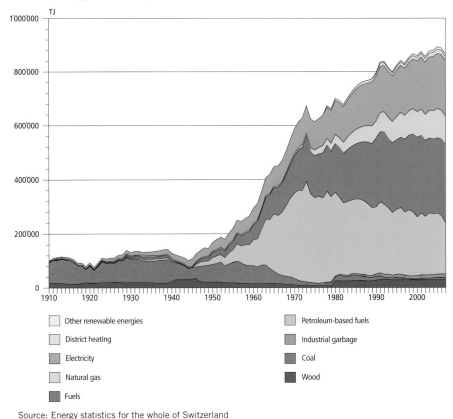

Source: Energy statistics for the whole of Switzerland

Other renewable energies	Petroleum-based fuels
District heating	Industrial garbage
Electricity	Coal
Natural gas	Wood
Fuels	

Hydroelectric power stations by canton					
Canton	Power stations	Installed capacity in MW = 1000 kW	Canton	Power stations	Installed capacity in MW = 1000 kW
Valais	87	4'622	St. Gall	44	421
Grisons	84	2'640	Glarus	29	471
Ticino	30	1'448	Argovia	23	483
Berne	62	1'307	Uri	21	488

Source: DETEC - Federal Office of Energy, Hydroelectric Section 2008

renewable energies. Important renewable energy sources are solar energy for hot water or electricity, cogeneration of heat and power in order to use ambient heat, biogas or bio-mass-based fuel. The largest "alternative" energy source, with just under a 4% share, is the burning of refuse. The production of energy from hydroelectric power stations is also being further extended. The future of nuclear energy remains an open question, although the ten-year moratorium on the construction of new nuclear power plants expired in 2000. Electricity consumption is still increasing constantly.

The environment must be respected through a more efficient use of energy and the country's dependence on oil must be further reduced. Whereas Switzerland's petroleum supply has, from the beginning, been provided by the private sector, gas, water and electricity utilities belong, with a few exceptions, to municipalities or cantons. A law for liberalised market structures and (partially) privatised energy companies is gradually being implemented – but not without protests.

Despite the environmental targets, direct incentives for renewable energies remain the exception in Switzerland, however. In addition, subsidies are suffering under pressure from the State to economise. One important target which is laid down in the Energy Act, but which has been partially overlooked politically, is to reduce CO_2 emissions by 10%, in comparison with 1990, by the year 2010. The aim is to achieve a reduction of 10% in the consumption of fossil energies and a maxi-mum 5% increase in electricity consumption. For the time being, the aim is to achieve this by voluntary agreements with business and industry. If the target is not achieved with these, control taxes like the CO_2 tax or the "climate cent" which has been introduced for fuels will be imposed on CO_2 emissions. The proportion of renewable energies is to rise by one per cent for electricity and by three percentage points for heat generation.

These small steps are being taken by Switzerland against the background of worldwide efforts to promote sustainable energy policy. In the "Kyoto Protocol", which was signed by most states, similar targets were agreed internationally. Resistance from business and laziness on the part of individuals often stand in the way of the aim of economical and environmentally acceptable use of energy. www.energie-schweiz.ch

Oil

In Switzerland as elsewhere, the oil crisis of 1973 brutally demonstrated the vulnerability of energy supplies of countries with no mineral resources of their own to exploit. As a result of low prices, the proportion of Switzerland's energy consumption accounted for by oil had risen from 24% (1950) to nearly 80%. Since then it has fallen to 55 per cent – and the marked price increase of oil in 2008 should reduce consumption again. Since Switzerland possesses no oilfields, oil must be imported, either as refined products (not quite two thirds) or crude oil. The latter is transformed into finished products, around 50% motor fuel and 50% heating fuel, at the refineries in Cressier (Canton of Neuchâtel) and Collombey (Valais). Branch lines connected to the European pipelines had to be constructed to supply these refineries. Almost half of the crude oil processed was produced in Libya, and another third in Nigeria.

Energy supplied by hydroelectric and nuclear power stations

Almost a quarter of the energy consumed by business and private households is electricity. In 2005, 60% of domestic electricity production derived from hydroelectric power. There are currently some 1'300 power stations. The turbines of the 513 larger stations, with an output of more than 300 kW, produce around 35'000 Gigawatt hours each year. In 1969

Switzerland entered the atomic age with the Beznau I nuclear power plant (Argovia). This was followed by the four nuclear power stations Beznau II, Mühleberg (Berne), Gösgen (Solothurn) and Leibstadt (Argovia) They generate 40% of Switzerland's electricity. Plans for several power stations, among them the particularly controversial plant at Kaiseraugst (Argovia) just outside Basle city, have been abandoned owing to the fierce opposition to nuclear energy.

Natural gas

Since natural gas was introduced in Switzerland in the early 1970's, its consumption has steadily risen. Switzerland is linked to the European transport network via 12 international supply channels. Gas now accounts for more than 12% of the final energy consumption. For many years now natural gas has been Switzerland's third largest source of energy.

Service industries

Since the end of the 19th century Switzerland has seen the development of a diversified service industries sector. This has been triggered by two things: a need for a high degree of security and a large volume of goods in transport - high values are insured and corresponding risks are covered for the domestic market, export or in transit, which has encouraged the growth of insurance companies. Banks and asset management companies have also flourished, on the one hand due to their proverbial reliability, but also because of the banking secrecy expressly protected by law.

The infrastructure for (tele)communications and traffic is also well developed. This also benefits tourism, an important source of foreign currency for the mountain regions in particular. In addition, training centres have long been a Swiss speciality.

Banks

The Swiss are traditionally reputed to be thrifty. There are approaching 19 million savings accounts with banks, statistically almost three per inhabitant. With the material wealth it brings, important foreign relations, high level of political and monetary stability and a great deal of experience in financial dealings, a dense network of bank branches sprang up. At the end of 2007 –

Swiss banking in figures (in billions)

Group of banks (Figures at end of 2007)	Number of institutes	Balance sheet total[2]	Fiduciary transactions[2]	Net profits[2]
Cantonal banks	24	356,6	9,94	2,63
Major banks	2	2'341,1	81,07	2,85
Regional and savings banks	76	85,3	0,67	0,51
Rural banks[1]	1	123,1	0,34	0,70
Other banks	61	199	78,71	2,72
Foreign-controlled banks (incl. branches)	122	288,8	258,27	3,78
Private bankers	14	29,5	46,16	0,46
Total	300	3'457,9	482,95	14,1

[1] Association with 390 affiliated local member banks   [2] in billions of francs

Source: Swiss National Bank

before the global financial crisis – there were 330 banks with 3'834 branches (3'517 in Switzerland and 317 abroad) and a good 136'000 employees. The banks' aggregate balance sheet total in Switzerland rose to the record value of 3'457,9 billion francs in 2007. Mortgages totalling CHF 665 billion were provided. And the CHF 5'402,8 billion of assets held in customers' securities deposits far exceeded the balance sheet transactions.

Like Swiss industry, the banks operate worldwide. There are 317 foreign branches; conversely 122 banks which are controlled by foreign companies exist in Switzerland. The balance sheets also reflect the degree of integration; more than half of the credits originate abroad and there are far greater liabilities in relation to foreign customers than to domestic ones. In addition, trustee transactions amounting to CHF 483 billion are carried out. It should be noted that the assets are mainly invested in western industrialised countries, while the principal sources of trustee liabilities, i.e. money deposited with Swiss banks, are developing countries and so-called off-shore financial centres.

Switzerland is zealous about its good reputation as a financial centre and is therefore extremely concerned about keeping funds originating from criminal activities away from its financial centres and thus protecting its reputation. A comprehensive defence system exists in the field of money laundering, which is regularly adapted to take account of developments in this field. The independent "Financial Action Task Force on Money Laundering (FATF)" states in its reports that Switzerland has developed extremely effective measures against criminal abuse. Various elements of the Swiss system have served as a model for other countries and institutions, including the Basel Committee's "1988 Code of Conduct on the Prevention of Money Laundering", the 40 recommendations of the FATF and the EU directive against money laundering. In addition, the Federal Council decided in March 2009 that Switzerland intends to adopt the OECD standard on administrative assistance in tax matters in accordance with Article 26 of the OECD Model Tax Convention. The decision will permit the exchange of information with other countries in individual cases where a specific and justified request has been made. Banking secrecy will, however, continue to exist.

The Swiss National Bank (SNB) is Switzerland's central banking institution. Its tasks are set out under article 99 of the Federal Constitution: "As an independent central bank the SNB shall pursue a monetary and exchange policy that serves the overall interests of the country; it shall operate under the supervision of the federal authorities."

www.snb.ch

www.swissbanking.org (Swiss Bankers' Association)

www.ebk.admin.ch

(Swiss Federal Banking Commission)

Insurance

That the Swiss are among the best insured people in the world is proverbial. As in other rich countries the demand for safeguarding against risks and protection of assets is high. The Federal Government spends around a quarter of its budget on social security and other insurance schemes as well. The private industry consists of 168 insurance companies, 117 of them providing property insurance against loss or damage, 26 providing life insurance and 25 being exclusively reinsurers. In 2007, the industry's income from premiums amounted to 21,3 billion francs for property insurance against loss or damage and 28,7 billion francs for life insurance. In terms of insurance premiums per capita, Switzerland ranks 4th internationally. On the other hand, the size of Switzerland's insurance market plays a relatively minor role (ranked 8th in Europe), due to the country's small population. 47'505 people are employed in the insurance sector. Two Swiss institutions rank among the twenty largest insurance companies in Europe, namely Zurich and Swiss Life.

www.svv.ch (Swiss Insurance Association)

Transport and communications

With respect to both rail and road transport, Switzerland remains a crossroads for many areas of Europe. As early as Roman times the passes in the Grisons linked Italy and the Germanic countries, the Great St. Bernard Pass connected Italy with Gaul and good roads ran between Lake Constance and Lake Geneva. In the 12th century, the St. Gotthard was surmounted. Tunnels have been built through four of the major Alpine passes. The 17 km-long Gotthard Tunnel, opened in 1980, is at present the second longest road tunnel in the world. The Vereina railway tunnel under the Flüela Pass, which has been in operation since November 1999, quickly and safely transports the train together with cars through to the Engadine in winter.

Switzerland has a high vehicle density. Over 5 million motor vehicles, ranging from tractors to cars and lorries to motorcycles are registered, including 3,9 million private cars. This is equivalent to 523 cars per 1000 inhabitants. Approximately 81% of all households have at least one car, 31% even have several cars. Rail travel is also popular, the infrastructure and rolling stock are constantly renewed, the rail network is well developed and covers about 3'000 kilometres. In total, Swiss Federal Railways SBB carried more than 300 million passengers in 2007. Of Swiss rail users, approximately 350'000 people have annual season tickets, valid for more or less the whole network, and more than two million have half-price tickets.

The annual mobility of the Swiss people is 19'000 km per person within the country and

Pass roads in the Alps

	Altitude m	Length km		Altitude m	Length km
Umbrail	2'501	33	San Bernardino	2'065	32
Nufenen	2'478	36	Road tunnel	1'644	6,6
Great St. Bernhard	2'469	79	Oberalp	2'044	32
Road tunnel	1'924	5,8	Simplon	2'005	46
Furka	2'431	28	Klausenpass	1'948	47
Flüela	2'383	26	Lukmanier	1'916	48
Bernina	2'323	33	Maloja	1'815	43
Albula	2'312	23	Col de la Croix	1'780	18
Julier	2'284	43	Lenzerheide	1'549	28
Susten	2'224	46	Col du Pillon	1'546	42
Grimsel	2'165	33	La Forclaz	1'527	20
Ofenpass	2'149	36	Jaun	1'509	39
Splügen	2'113	39	Col des Mosses	1'445	33
St. Gotthard	2'108	27	Brünig	1'007	19
Road tunnel	1'175	16,9			

abroad. Of this, just under 11'000 km are travelled by car, 3'400 km by air, 2'800 km by rail and approximately 750 km by cycle and on foot. In terms of time, the Swiss population spends 88 minutes travelling each day, of which 40 minutes is on foot or cycling.

www.uvek.admin.ch
(Federal Department of the Environment, Transport, Energy and Communications)

www.bav.admin.ch
(Federal Office of Transport)

www.astra.admin.ch
(Swiss Federal Roads Authority)

Problems facing Swiss transport policy

After the railway boom in the 19th century, the motor car dominated the period after the Second World War. A referendum held in 1960 approved the construction of an extensive network of national highways, integrating with the European motorway network. As of 2015, 1'858 km of expressways, mostly four-lane, should be available: they will have cost some CHF 70 billion. 90% of them are already in use. In addition to motorways, the

Swiss Federal Roads Authority manages a total of 2'300 km of main roads, more than 3'000 bridges, more than 200 tunnels and a multitude of avalanche screens and protective structures.

At the end of the 1960's the authorities adopted the idea of a comprehensive transport concept although it was only ten years later that a report was submitted by the Federal Commission. It advocates the targeted promotion of public transport, not least for reasons of environmental protection, in order to raise the proportional level of rail transport. The dense network of roads, railway lines, shipping and other means of transport, extending into the most remote of mountain regions, reflects the country's central position in Europe, boosts tourism and generally aids the economy. A clear barrier to further growth in road traffic passing through the Alps was created by the "alpine initiative", which was, surprisingly, accepted in a referendum. In order to protect the Alps from the negative impact of transit traffic, two measures are to be taken and implemented: firstly, relocating transit freight traffic from road to rail and, secondly, dispensing with the expansion of the capacity of the transit roads. The performance-related Swiss heavy vehicle tax was introduced in Switzerland on 1.1.2001 (Swiss Heavy Vehicle Tax Law). It was the first heavy vehicle tax in the world to apply to all lorries on all the roads of a country. A tax is levied on the basis of the kilometres driven, the total weight and the emissions level in order to cover the infrastructure costs and the external traffic costs. The "polluter pays" principle is therefore being applied, namely that the party causing the general public to incur costs must also bear these costs.

Leisure traffic by car is also increasing as previously. The more time passes, the more necessary it becomes for traffic planning and implementation to take account of protection against emissions as well as consideration for the remaining areas of natural beauty and for ecological diversity. In addition, despite all the efforts made, the flood of cars and trucks is also causing many accidents in Switzerland. The number of road fatalities is falling each year and is less than 400. A comprehensive set of measures, "Via Sicura", intended to make traffic even safer, is aimed at further reducing the number of victims.
www.uvek.admin.ch
www.voev.ch (Public transport)

The Swiss National Road System

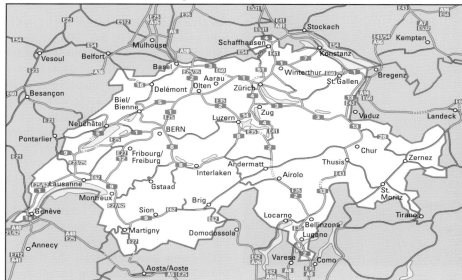

Source: Federal Roads Authority

No other country transports as much freight by rail as Switzerland (as shown here on the Gotthard route). The increasing transfer of heavy traffic from the roads to the railway – especially over long distances – is one of the focal points of Swiss transport policy. In particular, the motorways and roads crossing the Alps should be relieved of freight traffic. The "piggyback" rail service is used to transport lorries by rail.

Railways

The promotion and renewal of public transport were secured in the '90s. A whole package of measures was planned, under the title "Rail 2000", to guarantee faster journey times, better timetables and more comfortable travel thanks to new rolling stock. The largest but also the most expensive expansion in rail travel at the moment is the New Alpine Transversal (NEAT). The Simplon double-track tunnel was constructed in 1906. This will now be followed by the construction of low altitude tunnels, which will be single-track in places, under the Gotthard and Lötschberg Passes - for several billion francs. Since 2008 trains have been travelling through the 35 km long Lötschberg tunnel, from 2015 onwards through the Gotthard tunnel which, at 57 km long, will be the world's longest tunnel, at speeds of up to 250 kph. A further financial bill introduced in 1998 will cover the modernisation of the railway network, large sections of which date back to the 19th century. The railways will thus be able to deal with the problem of noise as well as integrating Switzerland into the European high-speed railway network. The TGV connection to Paris or the ICE to Hamburg are already a permanent fixture in the timetable.

The public sector financed rail transport in 2007 to the tune of over 2 billion francs, of which 1,3 billion alone went into the operation, preservation and maintenance of the infrastructure.

An important role in the "public transport" sector is played by the private railways with their network of around 2'000 km. Many of these are narrow gauge (1 m) and operate in mountain areas, such as the Rhaetian Railways or the Matterhorn-Gotthard line (Zermatt-Disentis). Others, such as the RBS (Berne-Solothurn regional railway), quickly realised the advantages of a dense timetable of regular trains. Like the privately owned rail companies, numerous aerial cableways and chairlifts are of great importance to tourism. Some 750 km of transport routes lead to many scenic mountains in Switzerland.

www.alptransit.ch (Alpine tunnels)
www.sbb.ch
www.litra.ch (SBB and other railways)
www.seilbahnen.org (Aerial cableways)

Busy shipping

26 shipping companies with many shipping lines on lakes and rivers stimulate tourism. This is especially true of the popular restored steam-driven paddle ships. Switzerland has a link to the sea via the Rhine. This route is used mainly for transporting bulk goods of all kinds as well as containers. An important part of foreign trade is conducted, in the true sense of the word, via the Basle Rhine ports (11% by tonnage). Imports of oil and oil products, as well as iron, steel and other metals, are transported by ship.

Not one centimetre of sea coast belongs to Switzerland. And yet an ocean-going fleet of 25 ships sails under its flag, which puts the country in the top half of the world's 152 seafaring nations. Since foreign merchant fleets would be under threat in times of war and international crises could severely reduce the tonnage of goods shipped, Switzerland passed a maritime shipping law in 1953. In recent years the very modern fleet has grown significantly and now has a load capacity of just under 800'000 DW tonnes (dead weight).

The "Gallia" which dates back to the era of the saloon steamers in the early part of the last century (year of construction 1913) operates to a regular timetable on Lake Lucerne. The ship was returned to service in 2004 following a comprehensive restoration. With a top speed of 31,44 kilometres per hour, it ranks as the fastest paddle steamer on a European lake. The popular veteran ship weighs 329 tonnes, has a length of 60 metres and can carry 900 persons.

Air traffic

Following the terrorist attacks in 2001, fatal accidents in Switzerland and the grounding of "Swissair", the Swiss civil aviation industry suffered a serious crisis: passenger numbers at Switzerland's three largest airports, Zurich, Geneva and Basle-Mulhouse, located on French territory, had fallen dramatically and countless suppliers and ancillary aviation companies found their existence was threatened. In the meantime, the situation has improved: thanks to support from government and industry, the airline "Swiss" was set up. "Swiss" is now a subsidiary of the German Lufthansa Group. The ancillary aviation companies and airports are back on the road to growth. The restrictions imposed by Germany since 2003 on the use of Southern German airspace have placed considerable strain on Zurich airport, with the additional aircraft constituting a burden to those living around the airport.

Post and telephones

Since 1st January 1998 "Die Post" (Swiss Post) with "Postfinance" and Swisscom have been developing as independent companies. Whereas Swiss Post is still fully state-owned, in October 1998 the Confederation sold over a third of its Swisscom shares to private investors. The question of whether Swisscom should be completely privatised and what role the Confederation is to play as the main shareholder has produced violent political discussions. It is still the case that a good basic service is provided, extending right into remote regions and the outlying districts of towns and cities. This "public service" is especially important for older people who are not (no longer) mobile and for people who do not have a car. "Public service" is also the key word for the post and public transport. At Swiss Post, 45'000 men and women ensure that approximately 2'750 million items of surface mail and 109 million parcels are delivered each year. The number of items of surface mail transported has been reducing since 2002, as a result of competition from new providers in the soon to be totally liberalised markets and electronic data transfer. The population sticks on almost 500 million stamps as postage, with a recent addition being "stamps" created and printed out via the Internet. However, only approximately 10'000 people still collect stamps. The network of 2'500 post offices has been shrinking for some time, but new forms are slowing this decline. However, 20'000 post-boxes also need to be designed to make them more secure and more practical.

In payments, too, Swiss Post is one backbone of the Swiss economy: through the 3,3 million Post Office accounts, payment transactions totalling 1,5 trillion francs are handled each year – approximately 60% of Swiss payments. The yellow postal buses, which have been transporting numerous commuters and tourists around the postal bus transport network, which now covers some 10'000 km, since 1906, remain an unmistakable part of the postal service. It is not just children's hearts which beat when the postal bus is heard approaching. The notes C sharp, E and A in A major originate from Andante from the overture of Gioacchino Rossini's "William Tell" opera. www.post.ch

Liberalisation has resulted in the state telecommunications provider – now called Swisscom – undergoing a far-reaching transformation into a modern service company.

Despite many reductions in tariffs and competition from new providers, particularly Sunrise and Orange, Swisscom remains well ahead of its competitors in terms of turnover (CHF 11 billion in 2007). And unlike most European telecoms companies, it does not have a high level of debt, but instead it is highly profitable.

There is a hard political and legal fight to secure the release of the "last mile", the metres of cable up to the individual household's connection. Swisscom operates, throughout Switzerland, a dense voice, mobile telephone and data network which still includes over 8'000 telephone boxes, and ensures optimum satellite communications. ISDN digital transmission technology is fairly widespread. The subsidiary Bluewin provides transmission of radio and television broadcasts via an extensive network of transmitters.

The mobile telephone network covers almost all of the inhabited corners of Switzerland. More than 90% of the inhabitants have a mobile telephone, in spite of the fears about the possible consequences of being subjected to electromagnetic rays and the resistance to new aerials. It is no longer possible

The first postal bus route started in 1906 in the Berne region. Today, yellow postal buses cross the Alps, provide a service for schoolchildren and commuters in many locations or open up isolated mountain valleys. Often the drivers drive past imposing cliffs or deep chasms with only a few centimetres to spare, as here in Bergell.

Tranquillity or impressive natural features (top: Aletsch Glacier, bottom: Pfäffikersee) and unspoilt natural habitats are among Switzerland's tourist assets. Considerate behaviour by tourists and recreational sports enthusiasts helps to keep them intact.

to imagine everyday life in Switzerland without mobile telephones. Short electronic text messages (SMS) are particularly popular and practical, with millions being sent each day. **www.swisscom.com**

Tourism

Thanks to its geographical location, Switzerland has always been a favourite travel destination – whether for merchants, Roman pilgrims or, since the 19th century, nature-loving tourists, who were seeking food and accommodation. The tracks were developed for them and as routes for the Säumer, the first people to transport goods across the Alps.

Since the 18th century literature and painting have aroused enthusiasm for the alpine world and thus acted as an altogether essential stimulus to tourism in Switzerland. It is now a question of preserving these "natural assets" of healthy air, a wide variety of scenery and peace. With almost 225'000 employees and 30'000 businesses, the hotel and restaurant business is one of the most important sectors in the economy of Switzerland, particularly in the outlying and mountainous regions.

Tourism contributes more than 6% of Switzerland's GDP. It is not just restaurants and the hotel and parahotel businesses which profit from visitors; indirectly, many other sectors live off tourism. In 2007, the number of overnight stays in Swiss hotels totalled 36,4 million. Conversely, Swiss citizens also really enjoy travelling. On average, they make 2,7 trips per year per person, with every ninth trip being a business trip. Retired people make significantly less trips involving overnight stays and 26-45 year olds cover the largest distances. Another key factor of how much people travel is their income. Those persons earning a higher than average monthly salary travel approximately twice as frequently and three times as far as others.

Switzerland's tourist infrastructure encompasses places with marked winter or summer tourism, biseasonal areas, spa resorts and congress centres. Since the end of the Second World War, rising incomes, the growth of motorisation and urbanisation have boosted tourism. Winter sport in particular has expanded strongly. As a result, a network of tourist railways and roads has sprung up and the number of beds in chalets and holiday apartments has grown. Demand is strongly governed by the exchange rate of the Swiss franc and the economic situation.

In order to give Switzerland a better profile as a travel destination, the tourism organisations, from Switzerland Tourism (ST) to numerous regional and local organisations, undertake major advertising initiatives. The economically fast growing, emerging countries, such as India, Russia or China are deliberately being targeted.

www.myswitzerland.com (Swiss Tourism)

The most important capital of tourism remains the landscape, both "untouched nature" and the cultural landscape shaped over centuries by agriculture. The tourism and construction industries nevertheless repeatedly call for additional infrastructure (roads, ski-lifts, car parks, etc.) and holiday homes. This meets with opposition, because such intervention always has an adverse effect on the landscape. In recent years, Switzerland has experienced relatively mild winters with little snowfall, which is why more and more ski resorts are investing in snowmaking systems costing millions of francs.

Hotel guests from within Switzerland and abroad

Canton	Number of nights' stays in hotels 2007			
	Swiss guests	Foreign guests	Total	Proportion of Swiss guests
Grisons	2'918'781	2'948'994	5'867'775	49,7%
Berne	2'238'688	2'764'755	5'003'443	44,7%
Valais	2'008'790	2'415'939	4'424'729	45,4%
Zurich	1'151'235	2'991'289	4'142'524	27,8%
Ticino	1'502'817	1'252'834	2'755'651	54,5%
Geneva	561'723	2'315'889	2'877'612	19,5%
Vaud	891'628	1'643'378	2'535'006	35,2%
Lucerne	618'499	1'119'754	1'738'253	35,6%
St. Gall	616'212	466'901	1'083'113	56,9%
Basle-Town	259'655	684'167	943'822	27,5%
Argovia	352'105	363'296	715'401	49,2%
Obwalden	253'849	383'518	637'367	39,8%
Schwyz	390'711	241'013	631'724	61,8%
Fribourg	227'665	158'445	386'110	59,0%
Thurgovia	241'152	156'165	397'317	60,7%
Solothurn	196'163	173'691	369'854	53,0%
Nidwalden	101'159	135'802	236'961	42,7%
Uri	88'847	169'465	258'312	34,4%
Neuchâtel	109'821	119'101	228'922	48,0%
Zug	136'691	128'485	265'176	51,5%
Basle-Country	109'647	106'151	215'798	50,8%
Appenzell I. Rh.	132'851	28'060	160'911	82,6%
Glarus	109'441	28'645	138'086	79,3%
Appenzell Out. Rh.	108'439	41'193	149'632	72,5%
Schaffhausen	51'977	70'676	122'653	42,4%
Jura	68'519	10'129	78'648	87,1%
Total	15'447'065	20'917'735	36'364'800	42,5%

Source: Federal Statistical Office

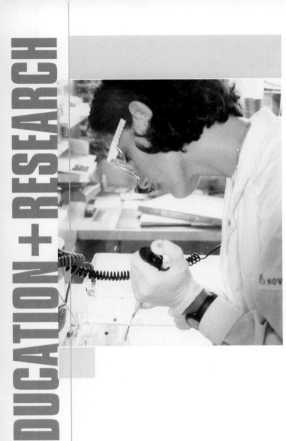

DIVERSITY AND QUALITY

In Switzerland, responsibility for education is shared between the federal authorities, the Cantons and the communes. The responsibilities vary according to the educational level and the educational establishment involved. The nationwide cooperation between the Cantons takes place largely through the Swiss Conference of Cantonal Ministers of Education (EDK). Improving the cooperation within the educational system is a continual process, which safeguards the quality of the educational system and facilitates pupil mobility. As a result, Switzerland is able to occupy as high a position as possible in the international league table. However, regional and local traditions and identities are to be retained.

www.swissworld.org

From pre-school to university

Switzerland attaches great importance to the quality of its education system. The main responsibility for pre-school, primary and lower secondary schooling is in the hands of the Cantons and their communes. This means that consideration is also given to the varied cultural and linguistic needs of the respective Cantons. School entry age, the start and end of the school year and the length of compulsory schooling are uniformly regulated at national level.

A new Intercantonal agreement, the Harmos Concordat, is intended to further harmonise compulsory schooling. Each Canton will decide individually on the introduction of Harmos. The aim of Harmos is to maintain quality standards and free interchange between the compulsory schools and to remove barriers to mobility between schools. In future, nursery school attendance is to be compulsory. From age 4, children will be required to attend a nursery school or a so-called entry level (basic level). The first school level, including the entry level, is to last eight years, the secondary level three years.

The years of compulsory schooling are followed by the upper secondary school system which covers education under the headings of vocational training and general education (grammar schools, specialised colleges of further education). At the upper secondary school level, responsibility for the public education system is shared by the Cantons and the Confederation. Vocational training is controlled by the Confederation while the Cantons decide on its implementation and bear the lion's share of the costs. The Cantons and the Confederation jointly administer the baccalaureate, the Cantons run the grammar schools. Any other general education establishments at this level are the responsibility of the Cantons. **www.bbt.admin.ch, www.edk.ch**

In the university area as well as in the remainder of the tertiary area, responsibility lies to some extent with the Cantons and to some extent with the federal authorities. Switzerland is involved in the creation of a competitive and dynamic university and research area in Europe. It has introduced the two-tier system of studies with the Bachelor's Degree as the first level and the Master's Degree as the second. In addition, study achievements are recognised in accordance with the credit point system (ECTS) used throughout Europe.

Pre-school stage

A distinction is made in Switzerland between pre-school education (nursery school) and childcare outside the family (day nurseries, child-minders and play-groups). There is no statutory entitlement to childcare outside the family. However, in all of the Cantons children have a right to pre-school education for at least one year or even two years in half of the Cantons. A number of Cantons are already experimenting with the introduction of a so-called "Basic level". In this level, the nursery school years are amalgamated with the first school years. This level is attended by four to eight-year-olds who are able to join and leave on a flexible basis according to their development.

Compulsory schooling

Children start school no earlier than 6 years of age. Compulsory schooling – primary schooling and lower secondary schooling – lasts nine years and is free of charge for the pupils. In most Cantons children may attend school voluntarily for a tenth year. Primary schooling lasts six years in the majority of Cantons, followed by three years of lower secondary schooling. In six Cantons schooling is subdivided into four and five years or five and four years. At lower secondary school level, children are generally divided into groups with different requirements. Depending on the type of school, it is possible to move between groups. Childcare over lunchtimes and outside school lessons is offered as an additional service at some schools.

Post-compulsory education

Following compulsory schooling, young people move into the upper secondary schooling. This is subdivided into the general education routes (grammar schools, specialised colleges of further education) and the vocational training routes. Upper secondary school courses last two to four years, with around 90 per cent of young people graduating from these.

The grammar schools generally prepare their pupils to go on to university. The examination subjects are made up of seven basic subjects combined with one selected main subject and one selected complementary subject. An assessment is also made of a major thesis which the student writes alone. The specialised colleges of further education prepare their students for advanced training schools and universities of applied sciences in the paramedical, social, educational and creative areas. The education at specialised colleges of further education up to final diploma level lasts three years. The Specialised Baccalaureate Certificate can be acquired through periods of practical training or attending additional lessons.

Around two thirds of young people in Switzerland complete a vocational training course after their lower secondary schooling. This can be undertaken in companies providing vocational training, complemented with one to two days' tuition per week in a vocational training college, or the trainees attend a full-time course of study such as a training workshop or full-time vocational college.

The two-year basic vocational training offers an opportunity for more practically oriented young people to obtain a recognised qualification with a federal vocational certificate. The three or four-year basic vocational training is completed with a Federal Capacity Certificate.

A choice of around 300 apprenticeships is available. The most popular apprenticeships are clerk, salesperson, retail sales assistant, chef and electrical fitter. During and after completion of an apprenticeship the "Vocational Baccalaureate" can be gained in the areas of technology, commerce, applied art, trade, science, health and social affairs.

Admission to a university of applied sciences does not involve an entrance examination if the applicant has completed a "Vocational Baccalaureate" in combination with an apprenticeship in a profession related to the course of study. Holders of a "Vocational Baccalaureate" are also able to move on to a suitable university by passing a supplementary examination. **www.educa.ch**

Higher vocational education

Higher vocational education includes vocational examinations and advanced technical examinations as well as the advanced training schools ("Höhere Fachschulen"). Higher vocational education enables students to obtain qualifications at the tertiary level required to exercise demanding and responsible occupations. Examinations can be taken in more than 350 recognised trade and higher vocational subjects (master craftsman's examinations). The vocational examination is completed with a Federal Certificate of Higher Vocational Education, the higher vocational education and training examination with a diploma. The advanced training schools offer federally approved courses in the areas of technology, hotel trade, tourism and domestic science, economics, agriculture and forestry, health, social matters and adult education, arts and design. **www.bbt.admin.ch**

Universities

Switzerland has ten universities: four in French-speaking Switzerland (Fribourg, Geneva, Lausanne and Neuchâtel), five in German-speaking Switzerland (Basle, Berne, Lucerne, St. Gallen and Zurich) and one in Ticino (Lugano-Mendrisio). They offer courses in theology, humanities and social sciences, mathematics and natural sciences, law, economics, medicine and pharmacology. The two Federal Institutes of Technology in Lausanne and Zurich offer courses in natural and engineering sciences, architecture, mathematics and pharmaceutical sciences as well as sports and military sciences. Admission to the universities is by way of baccalaureate or equivalent qualifications.

In addition to the traditional tasks of research and training of new academic blood at the universities, their service functions (commissioned tasks, information) are gaining in importance. Approximately 25% of the young people living in Switzerland have a university degree, with just under 25'000 students graduating each year. Of these, two-thirds gain a diploma from a university, while the other third are awarded diplomas from universities of applied sciences.
www.swissuni.ch
www.epfl.ch
www.ethz.ch

Universities of Applied Sciences

The universities of applied sciences provide courses of study with a practical emphasis in the fields of technology and information technology, architecture, construction and planning, chemistry and life sciences, agriculture and forestry, economics and services, design, health, social work, art, music, theatre as well as applied psychology and applied linguistics. The Federal Vocational Baccalaureate is the main route for a course of studies at a university of applied sciences. Holders of a federally recognised matriculation baccalaureate have access to their chosen course of study without the need for an examination after one year's practical work experience in the area.
www.kfh.ch
(Conference of Universities of Applied Sciences of Switzerland)

Teacher training

Teachers for pre-school, primary and lower secondary schooling levels as well as for grammar schools are largely trained at teacher training colleges. These have the status of universities of applied sciences. As a general rule, admission to a course of studies at a teacher training college calls for a baccalaureate from a grammar school.

Teacher training is characterised by a high degree of practical relevance. On-the-job training is also an important part of the overall training in the fields of speech therapy, psychomotor therapy and remedial education. Teachers for vocational training colleges are trained at the Swiss Institute

IT professions are so popular among Swiss youngsters that the demand for training places frequently exceeds supply. On the other hand, professions such as cheese maker, butcher and baker often suffer from a lack of new recruits.

for Vocational Training. In future, vocational training instructors are to be trained at the Eidgenössisches Hochschulinstitut für Berufsbildung (Federal Higher Institute for Vocational Education).
www.sibp.ch (Swiss Institute for Vocational Training)

Further training

Further training comprises organised learning following the completion of the first stage of training. It is first and foremost the responsibility of private educational institutions and universities. Lifelong learning is becoming increasingly important at all levels of education. The annual expenditure for further training runs into the billions, the costs being paid principally by the participants but also partially by the companies.
www.w-a-b.ch
(further education opportunities)

Research and Development

Somewhat lacking in natural raw materials, Switzerland decided to concentrate at a very early stage on its qualities and skills

in the areas of education, research and technology in order to ensure its economic prosperity and competitiveness. With R+D expenditure running at 2,2% of the Gross Domestic Product, Switzerland is among the group of the five most research-intensive industrial nations. In comparison with other countries, an above-average proportion of the sector in Switzerland is financed by private industry. Of the CHF 9'660 million spent on R+D by Swiss private industry in the most recent survey carried out in 2004, three quarters was accounted for by the following four research-intensive branches of industry, that is to say the pharmaceutical and chemical industry (37%), the engineering and metal industry (16%), research laboratories (14%) as well as information and communication technologies (9%). In addition, Swiss groups invested over CHF 9'600 million abroad in research and development during 2004. The total invested abroad in R+D by Swiss private industry was therefore the same as it made available for R+D in its own country. The total demonstrates the extremely active participation of Swiss companies in international research projects. Switzerland is also involved in the realisation of a European Research Area. The R+D area is a major employer for Switzerland, providing jobs for approximately 38'000 people, 47% of whom have a university degree.

The Swiss National Science Foundation (SNSF) is the most important Swiss Institution for the promotion of scientific research. It promotes all disciplines, from philosophy through biology up to nano sciences and medicine. The SNSF, on behalf of the Federal Government, mainly supports basic research. In various areas, however, it also promotes research into practical applications. Every year, the SNSF supports over 7'000 scientists.

www.sbf.admin.ch (State Secretariat for Education and Research)
www.aramis-research.ch (The Swiss Research Information System)
www.psi.ch (Paul Scherrer Institute)

Several Nobel prizes for chemistry, physics and medicine have been awarded to researchers working at Swiss universities. Throughout the centuries, the universities have played a major role in the intellectu-al life of the country. The names of Erasmus and Paracelsus, as well as the theologian Karl Barth and the philosopher Karl Jaspers, who both became famous in the 20th century, are firmly linked with the University of Basle. In psychology, C.G. Jung introduced new ways of understanding the psyche with the notion of archetypes and the collective unconscious; and Jean Piaget, with his work in child psychology, gave us a clearer understanding of the notion of intelligence.

The Swiss Federal Institute of Technology of Zurich (ETH Zurich) was opened in 1855. 20'000 people from 80 nations study, carry out research or work there. Approximately 360 professorships are responsible for research and tuition, mainly in the technical subjects, mathematics and natural sciences. 21 Nobel prize winners are associated with the ETH Zurich.

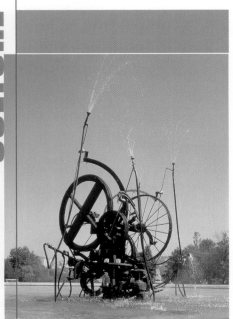

SWITZERLAND – A LAND OF CULTURE

Despite the small size of the country, Switzerland's cultural life is as intense as it is diverse. There are two main reasons for this cultural profusion. On the one hand, there is the linguistic diversity: four different languages are spoken in Switzerland and, in addition, numerous dialects. Three of the languages – German, French and Italian – are those of major European cultural areas. On the other hand, Switzerland's special geographical situation has always induced Swiss artists, patrons of the arts, theatre producers, etc. to also look beyond their own country and their creations have been enriched by visitors as well as emigrants.

www.swissworld.org

Cultural policy – the joint concern of the Confederation, Cantons and municipalities

Cultural life and cultural policy are played out in a finely-coordinated combination of action by the Confederation, Cantons and local authorities (municipalities or communes). The costs involved in cultural activity are borne primarily by private individuals, foundations, and by communes. The largest communes – that is, the country's major cities – meet more than half the cost of cultural life in Switzerland, although they represent less than a quarter of the total population.

Within the context of our federal state, the primary responsibility for culture at government level lies with the Cantons, which supplement the cities' efforts with their own investments. The Confederation divides its activities among various agencies which each have their own statutory basis or political mandate. The Confederation's promotion of culture in Switzerland is based on teamwork between the Federal Office of Cultural Affairs and the "Pro Helvetia" foundation. The cultural activities of Switzerland abroad are based on the cooperation of the Federal Office of Cultural Affairs, Pro Helvetia and the Federal Department of Foreign Affairs.

The Federal Office of Cultural Affairs

The Federal Office of Cultural Affairs is the Confederation's specialist authority for basic cultural policy issues, for the promotion of culture and for the preservation and conveyance of cultural values. It promotes cultural life in its diversity and creates the prerequisites to allow this to both develop and develop further independently. The responsibilities fulfilled by the Federal Office of Cultural Affairs are many and varied. They include the promotion of art and design, cinema, dance, the protection of cultural heritage and monuments, and support for various institutions and issues, including cultural umbrella organisations, Swiss schools abroad and the affairs of the linguistic minorities and travelling people as well as youth issues. It also runs the National Museum (Musée Suisse Group) and the National Library, which also includes the Swiss Literature Archive, established in 1991, and the Centre Dürrenmatt in Neuchâtel, which opened in 2001, the Federal Art Collections, the museum of the Oskar Reinhart collection "Am Römerholz" in Winterthur and the Museo Vela in Ligornetto (Ticino). **www.bak.admin.ch**

Pro Helvetia

Alongside the Federal Office of Cultural Affairs, Pro Helvetia is the Confederation's main agency for the promotion of culture and, as a public trust, is subject to the control of the Federal Department of Home Affairs and the supervision of the Federal Council. The mission of Pro Helvetia is, on the one hand, to promote cultural creation throughout Switzerland and to foster cultural exchange between the different parts of the country. On the other hand, the foundation helps to project Swiss cultural creation abroad. Its head office is in Zurich; since the autumn of 1992 a branch for French-speaking Switzerland has existed in Geneva. Pro Helvetia receives its financial resources from the Confederation, allocated to it by Parliament for four-year periods.
www.pro-helvetia.ch

Switzerland's new cultural constitution

Article 69 of the revised Federal Constitution, which became law on 1st January 2000, established an explicit basis for the

Open-air performances are an integral part of the Swiss cultural summer. These include performances of classical works such as the Classic Openair in Solothurn and the open-air opera performance in the Roman arena in Avenches (above) as well as internationally renowned rock and pop festivals and numerous city centre events. Left: Art also has a place in the open air: "La fontaine de Jo Siffert", a work in Fribourg by Jean Tinguely, the sculptor in iron.

The "Centre Dürrenmatt", designed by internationally known Swiss architect Mario Botta, high above Lake Neuchâtel, is dedicated to the major Swiss writer and dramatist Friedrich Dürrenmatt. The centre, which opened in the year 2000, is unique among cultural projects in Switzerland, illustrating the relationship between literature and the fine arts. Among other items, it shows films, film portraits, interviews and recordings of theatre performances, as well as pictures and caricatures by Dürrenmatt, who also drew and painted all his life.

Confederation's promotion of culture. Prior to that, constitutional articles did exist regarding the cinema, protection of nature and cultural heritage and languages.

Article 69 of the Federal Constitution stipulates that the field of culture is a cantonal matter. The Confederation may support cultural activities of national interest, and encourage art and music – in particular in the field of education. In accomplishing its tasks, it shall take into account the cultural and linguistic diversity of the country. The "cultural article" closes the legal loophole between the Constitution and the Confederation's actual promotion of culture. It constitutes the basis of the Act for the Promotion of Culture as well as the revision of the Pro Helvetia Act from 1965. Both laws were submitted by the Federal Council to Parliament on 8 June 2007 and should come into force in the near future. The cultural article provides an opportunity to rethink and reorganise the Confederation's cultural policy as well as its interaction with the Cantons, communes and private individuals.

www.kultur-schweiz.admin.ch

Fine Arts

From a geographic point of view, Switzerland is a platform and interface for three major cultural circles – Italian, French and German. This situation has left its mark on the history of fine arts in Switzerland. Equally important was the fact that Switzerland has no cultural centre of a size and influence that could have created a uniquely Swiss culture. Both of these facts resulted in Swiss culture being very outward looking, towards cultural metropolises such as Rome, Paris, Munich, London or, more recently, New York. Many artists were educated there, and a significant number established themselves there and achieved worldwide fame from those cities. For instance, Rome was where Ticino-born baroque artist Francesco Borromini (1599 – 1676) worked. The painter Johann Heinrich Füssli forged his career in London at the end of the 18th century as Henry Fuseli, at the same time as his compatriot Angelika Kauffmann. Arnold Böcklin built his reputation as a painter in Munich, Zurich and Florence in the second half of the 19th century. The artist and architect from Jura, Charles Jeanneret, better known as Le Corbusier, earned worldwide fame in the 20th century from his base in Paris, just like the sculptor and painter Alberto Giacometti from Bergell. Lastly, Fritz Glarner became one of the most important proponents of concrete art in New York.

Elements of a specific Swiss characteristic are first found in romanticism and its elevation of the Alpine nature and people to a national feature. Spurred by publications such as Albrecht von Haller's didactic poem "Die Alpen" (1735) and Jean-Jacques Rousseau's "Julie, ou la nouvelle Héloise" (1761), the Swiss Alpine landscape was discovered in the 18th century as the blueprint for wild and beautiful landscapes and unspoilt nature. From the pathos-filled Alpine landscapes of Caspar Wolf, François Diday and Alexandre Calame to the monumental mountain scenery of Giovanni Segantini and the mountainscapes and seascapes of Ferdinand Hodler, the region has been home to many of the best works of Swiss painting through to the 20th century.

A second element of a characteristically Swiss position comes from the diametrically opposite view, the urbane, internationally oriented outlook of the early modern artists. The Dada movement was born in 1916 in Zurich's "Cabaret Voltaire" with proponents such as Hugo Ball, Emmy Hennings, Hans Arp and Sophie Taeuber-Arp, Tristan Tzara and Marcel Janco. They were the start of a modern, "rational" attitude, which gained ground rapidly in all areas of the fine arts in Switzerland in the 1920s and 1930s. The key words are "Bauhaus" or "Neues Bauen", "Constructivism" or "Concrete Art". Alongside the Bauhaus masters Johannes Itten and Paul Klee, Max Bill and the "Zurich concrete artists" including Richard Paul Lohse, Camille Graeser and Verena Loewensberg were at the forefront. Through their work as painters, architects, book producers, designers and theoreticians, they made an essential contribution to enable modernism in Switzerland to survive the Second World War and ostracism by fascism, ensuring that Switzerland continued to be internationally regarded as a centre of constructive direction in art and design until the 1960s. Initiatives such as the

Alberto Giacometti (1901 – 1966) is one of the outstanding artists of the 20th century. The painter and sculptor came from a family of artists, grew up in Bergell in South Grisons and produced the majority of his paintings and sculptures in Paris. His work was influenced by cubism, surrealism, existentialism and phenomenology, and is dominated by his unceasing search for the essence of existence. Alberto Giacometti found fame with his sculptures featuring excessively long figures which were very thin and often very tall. The Kunsthaus in Zurich houses the most important and most extensive collection of his works.

A Swiss tour of a special kind: the Museum of Transport and Communication in Lucerne, one of Europe's major museums of the history of transport, presents an aerial image of Switzerland on a scale of 1:20'000. To discover the numerous details of the landscape, the public explores this scaled-down version of Switzerland, which occupies just under 200 m², on foot.

"Die gute Form" prize for modern, functional design products, awarded every year until 1968, supported the image of unfussy quality and concentrated care, typically Swiss characteristics. At the same time, Switzerland saw the birth of a unique, vital direction in iron sculpture, ranging from the objects of Walter Linck and Robert Müller to the kinetic machinery of Jean Tinguely and the massive iron colossi of Bernhard Luginbühl. Alongside them, more and more Swiss artists are finding the international spotlight; their work can scarcely be given one single label any more. A few examples worth mentioning are Eva Aeppli, Franz Gertsch, Rolf Iseli, Meret Oppenheim, Markus Raetz, Dieter Roth, Niki de Saint Phalle or Daniel Spoerri.

In the last 20 years, contemporary art in Switzerland has enjoyed a boom. Several factors are responsible for this: on the one hand, public and private support for art has seen a significant increase; new museums, art galleries and alternative exhibition spaces are springing up in many places. At the same time, the art trade, which has traditionally held a strong position in Switzerland, has also discovered young Swiss art and opened a window to it at international and world-renowned art fairs such as "Art" in Basle and Miami. Contemporary artists such as John Armleder, Silvie Fleury, Peter Fischli & David Weiss, Roman Signer, Pipilotti Rist or Thomas Hirschhorn have benefited from this situation and today are widely acclaimed artists on the international exhibition circuit.

The museums

There are over 950 museums in Switzerland. Some of these are small and a few are open only at irregular times. Considered in local and regional terms, however, they are important cultural factors, indispensable for preserving the distinctive features of a particular village or valley.

Most of the major museums in Switzerland belong to a local authority; a smaller number are operated by a Canton, a university, or a private or semi-public foundation. As a federal institution, the National Museum has collected, conserved and exhibited

The Swiss National Museum has collected, con-
served and exhibited cultural artefacts of all peri-
ods and from all areas of Switzerland since 1890.
Its main centre is in Zurich (above); the branch for
French-speaking Switzerland is at the Château de
Prangins near Nyon (centre).

The Swiss National Museum includes six further
museums: the Zunfthaus zur Meisen and the
Bärengasse Museum in Zurich, the "Swiss History
Forum" in Schwyz, the Swiss Customs Museum in
Cantine di Gandria in Ticino, the Museum of
Musical Automata in Seewen in the Canton of
Solothurn and Schloss Wildegg and its estate in the
Canton of Argovia.

The Museo Vela in Ligornetto in the Canton of
Ticino (above) is also operated by the Confederation. In 1863 the sculptor Vincenzo Vela who had
found fame in Italy had a grand house and studio
constructed in his home village. Today, the magnificent building, which is situated in its own grounds,
houses the works of several members of the Vela
family of artists.

The Paul Klee Centre, which was constructed on the eastern outskirts of Berne in accordance with the designs of the Italian architect Renzo Piano, has been dedicated since 2005 to the multidisciplinary activities of Paul Klee as a painter, musician, teacher, writer, philosopher and educationalist. The centre's offerings do not wish to appeal solely to the "artistic elite", but to a broad cross-section of the population. Among other things, the Paul Klee Centre houses a "Children's Museum" for people from 4-99 years of age.

cultural artefacts of all periods and from all areas of Switzerland since its foundation in 1890. **www.musee-suisse.ch**

Basle, Berne, Geneva and Zurich are the principal artistic centres in Switzerland, and have several renowned art collections. In addition to a superb collection of old art, Basle boasts a modern art collection of world importance. The Jean Tinguely Museum displays groups of works and machine sculptures by the Swiss artist; the modern museum building was designed by the Ticino architect Mario Botta. In the neighbouring municipality of Riehen, the Fondation Beyeler is also devoted to modern art: its first-rate artworks and alternating exhibitions attract an international public.

The various 20th century artistic movements in Europe and the USA are prominently represented in the Kunsthaus in Zurich, as is the Swiss art of the last two centuries. The Musée d'art et d'histoire in Geneva includes, apart from its departments devoted to history, a comprehensive collection of paintings with works of the 18th – 19th century Geneva School, Dutch and French paintings of the 16th – 18th centuries and Old Masters from Italy, Flanders and Swabia. The Bernese art museum exhibits Bernese painting from the 15th to the 20th century. The Paul Klee Centre opened its doors to an international public in 2005. The Oskar Reinhart collection "Am Römerholz" in Winterthur has a worldwide reputation. As well as pictures and drawings by old masters including by Cranach, Greco and Goya, it includes quite a lot of representative groups of works of important French painters and sculptors of the 19th century. Other collections and museums worth seeing in Switzerland include the Museum Rietberg in Zurich and the Musée de l'art brut in Lausanne. There are famous historical museums everywhere, the largest being those in Berne, Geneva and Basle. The Museum of Transport and Communication in Lucerne is one of the largest museums dedicated to the history of transport in Europe. The Technorama in Winterthur displays the history of technology from the 19th century to today. The International Clock Museum in La Chaux-de-Fonds houses a unique collection of more than 3'000 clocks. The open-air museum of Ballenberg near Brienz, which has a collection of farmhouses from all parts of the country, and the Museum of Communication in Berne are also of national interest.

A stage which holds up a mirror to the world

Swiss theatrical life can look back on a long and lively tradition. As early as the Middle Ages, religious plays such as Nativity and Passion Plays were performed in the Confederation. Towards the end of the 19th century, the popular theatre enjoyed a lasting revival: many works which were performed for the first time then are still staged today – such as the William Tell plays, based on Friedrich Schiller's drama, which are regularly performed in Altdorf and Interlaken. In Einsiedeln, Caldéron's "The Great Theatre of the World", staged every five years, continues the tradition of the mediaeval and baroque religious play.

The performances given during the "Fête des Vignerons" wine-growers' festival in Vevey on Lake Geneva are devoted to the theme of wine and wine-making. They were inaugurated at the end of the 18th century and are staged every 25 years – most recently in 1999. Since 1908, the "Théâtre du Jorat" in Mézières, in a rural setting near Lausanne, has been a well-known popular theatre.

Many of the productions staged by the major Swiss theatres in Basle, Berne, Geneva and Zurich are well-known far beyond the frontiers of Switzerland. The renown of the theatres in German-speaking Switzerland, especially Zurich, dates back to the period from 1933 to 1945, when prominent German dramatists, producers – among them Bertolt Brecht – and actors had fled to Switzerland from the National Socialist regime. A very fertile intellectual climate came into being in the theatre, bringing forth new talent, particularly Max Frisch and Friedrich Dürrenmatt, who were a major influence on the contemporary German-language theatre for many years. "Living Theatre" tours in the 1960s gave the theatre a new impetus from outside.

Alongside the major theatres, a small theatre scene, which is still growing, flourished in the 1960s. It has taken on an important function of theatrical life in

Massimo Rocchi, Italian-European Swiss national by choice and possessing dual passports, is one of the greats of the Swiss cabaret scene. He stands for word acrobatics and pantomimes, wit and drollery. In his Circo Massimo programme, he juggles with the idioms of Europe in Italian, French, German, Schwyzerdütsch and Spanish, satirises language clichés and caricatures every nation. Rocchi has received major awards in several European countries.

The Lucerne Festival is one of Europe's major classical music festivals. It takes place in late summer each year in Lucerne's Cultural and Conference Centre, designed by leading French architect Jean Nouvel. The programme includes a broad spectrum of classical music, from symphony concerts, chamber music and serenades to contemporary works.

Switzerland, not just in the major cities: In southern Switzerland and the Romansch-speaking area theatrical life is, apart from a few exceptions, largely dependent culturally on the neighbouring regions. In Verscio, at the entrance to the Centovalli (region with its "hundred valleys"), the internationally known clown Dimitri founded his own theatre which was later followed by a mime school.

A large number of itinerant circus and street theatre troupes perform throughout Switzerland. Numerous theatre festivals, e.g. the Zurich Theatre Festival, the Festival du Belluard in Fribourg and the Festival de la Bâtie in Geneva, are also an established feature of Swiss cultural life during the summer months.

A varied dance scene

For many years, Switzerland was largely a host country for foreign dancers. During the two world wars in particular, countless dancers and choreographers sought asylum in the Confederation. A few of them stayed and instilled a love of classical ballet in the public. Today there are seven so-called institutional ballets. In addition to these, an increasing number of free companies and solo artists have established themselves since the 1980s, contributing to a varied, lively and innovative dance scene. They currently number around 70. The Zurich Ballet under Heinz Spoerli is known worldwide. His choreography goes beyond the classical vocabulary and frequently incorporates contemporary elements. Maurice Béjart has also established himself on the international stage. He might be called the epitome of dance: he has been a ballet director for more than 50 years and is the extremely successful director of the Lausanne Ballet. The works of the former "enfant terrible" of the Swiss dance scene are popular both nationally and internationally: the choreography of Gilles Jobin from Lausanne is among the most innovative that Swiss dance has to offer. There are also many more established dancers and many promising newcomers. They captivate the public with their guest shows or at festivals such as the Berner Tanztage, the Oltener Tanztage, La Bâtie, Steps or the Zürcher Theaterspektakel. Swiss dance companies also enjoy considerable success abroad. Around 40 free and institutional companies perform more than 250 tours in more than 30 different countries on all five continents every year.

The magic of words...

Among the 19th century German-speaking Swiss authors who are read beyond the frontiers of Switzerland were Jeremias Gotthelf, Gottfried Keller, Conrad Ferdinand Meyer, Carl Spitteler and the children's author Johanna Spyri ("Heidi"). They were followed, at the beginning of the 20th century, by the representatives of so-called regional literature, the most familiar of whom is Meinrad Inglin.

The best-known German-speaking Swiss writers in recent times can be divided into three generations: the first wrote within the Swiss isolation enforced by National Socialism and Fascism and deepened by the Second World War. Their works are marked by a sense of confinement and patriotism in the sense of a national cohesion cemented by the political situation in Europe. Many authors, such as Robert Walser, fled into introspection, Others, such as Albin Zollinger, sought their own form of refuge in engagement with the outside world.

Max Frisch and Friedrich Dürrenmatt, whose works form a contribution to world literature, belong to the second generation of writers – those who began to write during the Second World War and benefited, after 1945 when the war ended and the borders opened, from the absolute cultural vacuum in Germany. This generation examines Switzerland intensively. Max Frisch criticises the Swiss scene in his novels. He reacts to this country, which he finds too confining, both in wartime and in peace, and provokes it.

Friedrich Dürrenmatt became famous as a dramatist. For him, the world can be expressed only through comedy; it brushes all social values aside and turns the familiar world upside down. Using the grotesque, Dürrenmatt takes up traditions from Antiquity and juggles social and political satire with a virtuoso's skill.

In the third generation, Swiss reality remains present, yet their work is more cosmopolitan: for Adolf Muschg, Hugo

Loetscher, Otto F. Walter, Peter Bichsel and Thomas Hürlimann Switzerland is a field of experimentation for social conflicts which could just as easily occur elsewhere. Others such as Beat Brechbühl, Erika Burkart, Jürg Federspiel, Franz Hohler or the poet Kurt Marti represent a multiplicity of literary forms of expression.

The literature of French-speaking Switzerland has always concentrated largely on inner conflicts, contemporary events scarcely figuring in its scope. This introspective literature has left its traces in the literary culture of the Suisse Romande to this day, characterising, for instance, the work of Philippe Jacottet. The mainly Protestant university Cantons of Geneva, Vaud and Neuchâtel have a long literary tradition, in which the essay and the novel predominantly figure.

Charles Ferdinand Ramuz was the first author to break open the rigid forms of French literary language and to allow everyday language to come into its own. His work dominates the literature of French-speaking Switzerland in the first half of the 20th century. Some of his successors became celebrated beyond the confines of the Suisse Romande. Blaise Cendrars and Charles Albert Cingria made an essential contribution to contemporary French-speaking literature and, in particular, poetry, while Robert Pinget was one of the protagonists of the Nouveau Roman. Yves Velan has explored new ground in the use of language, as Joyce and Beckett had done before him. Jacques Chessex and Georges Borgeaud were awarded famous French literary prizes in the 1970s. Maurice Chappaz, a native of Valais, brought about a fundamental renewal in the literature of the Suisse Romande, with his œuvre which is impressive in its vitality, while Georges Haldas is considered a relentless analyst of contemporary life.

Women play a significant part in the literature of French-speaking Switzerland. They include Monique Saint-Hélier, Catherine Colomb, Corinna Bille, Alice Rivaz and Edith Boissonnas. Their novels and poetry are original and scarcely influenced by contemporary literary movements.

In the Italian- and Romansch-speaking regions of Switzerland conditions have not favoured the development of a literature enjoying recognition beyond its native region. Authors in Italian-speaking Switzerland are often strongly influenced by the culture of nearby Italy or Lombardy. In the 20th century, Francesco Chiesa was for many years the outstanding man of letters. He renewed the literature of Ticino, and brought it general recognition, by deriving new forms from the classic Italian literary idiom. The work of Piero Bianconi also opened up new ground for a new generation of authors. In "Albero genealogico" he deals with a central problem in the history of Ticino – emigration in the 19th and 20th centuries – which he pursues using family documents. In 1943, Felice Filippini was awarded the Lugano Prize. This prize was later conferred on Giorgio Orelli, whose poetry has its roots in the human and political reality of the present day: through his desire to go beyond appearances to the essential, he made the author's political and social commitment possible once again, and thus became a model for subsequent generations of writers. He was followed, as authors of regional importance, by Plinio Martini, Anna Felder and Giovanni Orelli.

There is no such thing as unified Romansch literature; it is divided into five clearly distinct dialects. In the Engadine and in the Münstertal Selina Chönz writes impressionistic novellas and Cla Biert writes short stories characterised by heightened poetic realism. Andri Peer is a leading author of short stories, poet and essayist, and the founder of contemporary Engadine poetry. In the Surselva region a few poets, among them Theo Candinas, are giving a new impetus to literature. With their works they are committed, above all, to the defence of the language of their homeland.

200 archives, estates and collections are preserved in the Swiss Literature Archive, opened in Berne in 1991. The following authors, among others, are represented: Corinna Bille, Hermann Burger, Erika Burkhart, Blaise Cendrars, Maurice Chappaz, Jacques Chessez, Friedrich Dürrenmatt, Jürg Federspiel, Friedrich Glauser, Hermann Hesse, Ludwig Hohl, Hugo Loetscher, Golo Mann, Niklaus Meienberg, Andri Peer, Carl Spitteler, Jean Starobinski, Rainer Maria Rilke and Otto F. Walter.

... and sounds

The music life of Switzerland is as diverse as the other cultural areas. Passed on from generation to generation for the most part, the folk music tradition is rich and has so far withstood the levelling out tendencies exerted by the mass media as far as possible. In addition to folk music, the federalist system and clubs, organisations and societies have also played their part in ensuring that many smaller communes have a brass band or choir, whilst every major city has orchestras. Efforts to reappraise the handed-down music academically and to preserve it for posterity are welcome, as are the various initiatives to use specifically Swiss instruments, e.g. the alpenhorn, in new ways and therefore give folk music a traditional contemporary "feel".

In the field of classical music two orchestras rich in tradition stand out, namely the Orchestre de la Suisse Romande and the Tonhalle-Orchester in Zurich. The cities of Geneva and Zurich are also at the forefront in the field of opera – they have their own Opera Houses which have an excellent reputation well beyond the frontiers of Switzerland.

The Zurich Ballet under the direction of Heinz Spoerli has gained international renown. The works of the dancer and choreographer include numerous new creations which have won international recognition. Not only does his ensemble make guest appearances at the Zurich Opera House, but it also dances to great acclaim on the world's most renowned stages: Paris, London, Barcelona, Tokyo, Cape Town, Warsaw, Moscow, etc. The picture shows the Zurich Ballet dancing Bach's Goldberg Variations.

Pioneers for contemporary music both in Switzerland and abroad were the conductor, Ernest Ansermet, at the start of the last century with the Orchestre de la Suisse Romande, and the patron and conductor, Paul Sacher, in Basle and Zurich in the second half of the 20th century. Numerous music festivals which mostly feature leading international musicians and orchestras in summer – and in particular the Lucerne Festival which is rich in tradition – are important as showcases for new music.

As well as Joachim Raff (1822-1882), Arthur Honegger was one of the first Swiss composers to receive international recognition. He settled in Paris around 1910, founded the "Groupe des Six" which formed the avant-garde of the time, together with Darius Milhaud, Francis Poulenc and others. Honegger, who never entirely broke with musical tradition, but also made no concessions to the masses, always took care that his music could be understood by the public. Later, Swiss composers, Othmar Schoeck and Frank Martin, found acclaim beyond the frontiers of Switzerland.

The composers of the following generation such as Armin Schibler, Robert Suter, Rolf Liebermann and Heinrich Sutermeister were influenced by them, each in his own way.

The youngest generation has already been able to draw, for its training, on a Swiss musical tradition. It is oriented, however, towards international movements and has detached itself from typically Swiss elements. They are musicians who are open to the great social and cultural problems of the present day: Klaus Huber, Ernst Pfiffner, Jürg Wyttenbach, Rudolf Kelterborn, Jacques Wildberger and Heinz Holliger who is esteemed equally as a composer and oboist.

Since the 1930s, jazz has been appreciated and cultivated in Switzerland. Many ensembles have become famous far beyond the frontiers of the country. In Berne, Lucerne and Zurich jazz schools train young jazz musicians. Internationally renowned jazz festivals are held annually in Montreux, Willisau, Berne, Zurich and Lugano.

Musical groups playing dialect rock have been enjoying success for around thirty years; they have made a considerable contribution to strengthening the use of dialect in everyday life and in the media.

Bands – with songs in dialect or other languages – are to be found even in small towns; some have even gained recognition beyond the frontiers of Switzerland.

There are also numerous rock and folk festivals; the Paléofestival in Nyon, the Gurtenfestival in Berne and the festivals in Frauenfeld and St. Gall are especially well-known.

Swiss film

The mass medium of film has the potential to make a decisive contribution to the cultural identity of a country. It comes as no surprise that multicultural Switzerland gives particular importance to national film production, recognises and promotes its status in the media age. As elsewhere in Europe, state subsidies make a fundamental contribution to independent film production in Switzerland too and are of vital significance for many festivals. Furthermore, the financial commitment of the Swiss radio and television company SRG SSR idée suisse plays an important role. It promotes film and television film production within the framework of a cooperation agreement, known as the "Pacte de l'audio-visuel". Cantons and communes are also involved in supporting the film industry.

The legal framework conditions for state support for the film industry have been under continual review since the 1950s. The Film Act of 1962 laid the foundations. A revised version came into force on 1st August 2002. This new Film Act provides for a progressive system of financial support for film, maintaining a balance between market liberalisation and quality. It is based essentially on two pillars: on the one hand, on a modern concept of direct support for film production which provides support both selectively and dependent on a film's success. It is also based, on the other hand, on a liberal market regulation which guarantees the preservation of diversity in the offering. These framework conditions form the basis for the state support policy goals, which are formulated for a three to five-year period and which set specific points of focus. The appropriateness and effectiveness of these support strategies are reviewed regularly and widely discussed.

The direction in which policy develops, as regards support for the Swiss film industry, therefore depends on all those involved in the adventure of Swiss film: on producers and technicians, on directors and script-writers, on film rental outlets and cinema owners, on the Federal administration and political decision makers. They must combine their particular points of view into a general perspective, in order to jointly develop and implement Swiss film policy.

The history of Swiss cinema can be simplified into four periods: silent film production in German-speaking Switzerland (1915-19), silent film production in the Suisse Romande (1919-24), the "old" Swiss cinema (1930-64) and the "new" Swiss cinema (since 1964). The older generation still has vivid memories of the Swiss films of the war and post-war years in particular, such as Franz Schnyder's film versions of Gotthelf's novels. The subsequent era of "new Swiss cinema" – the counterpart of the "nouvelle vague" in France – led to a radical artistic split and illustrated the different genre preferences between French- and German-speaking Switzerland. The German-speaking area concentrated on critical documentaries,

My name is Eugen (2005), a complex dialect adaptation of the Swiss children's classic by Klaus Schädelin, is set in 1960s Switzerland. With his adventurous comedy about the rascals Eugen, Wrigley, Bäschteli and Eduard, Michael Steiner appealed to the taste for indigenous drama.

Dutti der Riese [Dutti the Giant] (2007) deals with the career of the Swiss entrepreneur Gottlieb Duttweiler (1888-1962), also called "Dutti" for short. Duttweiler decisively changed and influenced consumer habits in Switzerland. Starting with a fleet of five vans in 1925, he laid the foundations for Migros which is now the largest retail company in Switzerland. Migros is everywhere and known to everybody in Switzerland. Duttweiler decreed that Migros had to invest a fixed amount of its turnover in cultural, sporting and leisure activities. This led to the establishment of the Klubschule Migros [Migros Club School] in the education field and various recreational facilities as well as the Gottlieb Duttweiler Institute.

while in the French-speaking regions preference was given to feature films. Similarities can, however, be seen in the choice of subject matter, since Swiss film makers of this time focused almost exclusively on life in their own country, with the existential contrasts in Switzerland and the ritualised expressions of life at home.

These universal concepts led Swiss cinema inevitably beyond the narrow national frontiers. The work of Alain Tanner, Claude Goretta, Michel Soutter, Jean-Louis Rey and Jean-Jacques Lagrange is as highly regarded abroad today as it was in the past. Yves Yersin also won international acclaim with "Les petites fugues". With "Höhenfeuer" ("Alpine Fire") Fredi M. Murer created a densely atmospheric masterpiece of worldwide renown and Xavier Koller was the first Swiss director to win an Oscar for Best Foreign Film with the refugee drama "Reise der Hoffnung" ("Journey of Hope") in 1991.

The domestic film industry is more alive than ever before. Alongside the established old masters, a younger generation of directors is seeking out new paths with unconventional choices of subjects, storytelling techniques and imagery, heralding the fifth phase of Swiss cinema. The past work of Jean-Stéphane Bron, Ursula Meier, Vincent Plüss, Manuel Flurin Hendry, Thomas Thümena, Anna Luif and many others offers a promise for the future. Michael Steiner's light-hearted children's book adaptation, "Mein Name ist Eugen" (My name is Eugen) (2005) set a Swiss box office record with more than 500'000 tickets sold. His economic thriller, "Grounding – die letzten Tage der Swissair" ("Grounding – the last days of Swissair") took an unconventional look at the many facets of an extraordinary corporate collapse and caused intense debate throughout Switzerland for weeks. French-speaking Swiss cinema has enjoyed international success with studies of human relationships: "Tout un hiver sans feu" ("All winter without fire") by Greg Zglinski was honoured at the Venice film festival in 2004. Lastly, Switzerland's characteristic genre, the documentary film, remains popular. The productions of Christian Frei (War Photographer, 2001; The Giant Buddhas, 2005) are particularly noteworthy here. The Swiss Film Prize has been awarded since 1998 as part of the annual Solothurn Film Festival. From 2009 onwards, this prize will be awarded in Lucerne.

Major Swiss film and video festivals are held annually in Locarno, Nyon, Fribourg, Baden and Basle.

www.swissfilms.ch
www.bak.admin.ch
www.filmtage-solothurn.ch
www.pardo.ch
www.visiondureel.ch

**THE MEDIA AND
MONITORING EVENTS**

The linguistic diversity and cultural structure of Switzerland have created a varied media scene. For financial reasons, however, the high degree of mediatisation is resulting in a continuous stream of mergers in the print media. A growing number of smaller newspapers are merging with major publishers in order to safeguard their existence. The national television and radio company encompasses eight television and 18 radio channels in the four national languages. Furthermore, the country has some 40 local and regional television stations and around 50 local and regional radio stations. A dense cable network means that the majority of Swiss households can receive at least 50 radio and television stations.

www.swissworld.org

Newspapers and magazines

There is no other country that has so many newspapers for such a small area as the multilingual Confederation of Switzerland. The number of daily papers has now fallen to 84, but over 200 newspapers are still available by subscription or over the counter with a total of around 3,8 million copies printed. This does not include club and association journals, official gazettes and free publications.

The large publishing houses, which are mostly multimedia companies involved in both printing and electronic communications, enjoy an increasing share of the market. The nine biggest newspapers (circulation of over 100'000) have more readers than the 200 odd smallest ones (circulation of up to 25'000) put together. Frequently, the smallest newspapers can satisfy niche markets as second newspapers. On the other hand, medium-sized daily papers are particularly under a great deal of pressure, because they are expected to offer a complete range of features which, however, given their limited financial means, they are less and less able to provide. Therefore, many newspapers are being taken over by large publishing companies and simply lend their title to a leading regional paper. However, a condensing of the market can be seen even in the case of the major publishing houses. For instance, in early 2009, the Zurich media publishing house, Tamedia, and Edipresse in Lausanne announced that they were merging their business in Switzerland. **www.schweizerpresse.ch**

Developments in advertising have an important influence on the rate of newspaper mergers and takeovers. Between 60 and 80% of revenue for subscription newspapers comes from advertising. Newspapers with a small circulation often find it more difficult as far as advertising is concerned because advertisers are mainly interested in the large circulation of a major newspaper in a certain area. Moreover, all print media have had to handle a radical change in the advertising market because small, classified advertisements (vehicles, accommodation and jobs) are increasingly posted on the Internet.

Most newspapers have turned their backs on their former ideological or party-orientated ties. Today, the typical Swiss daily newspaper is an independent publication offering news and points of view. It is the product of the increase in social awareness that Switzerland has seen over the past 30 years as well as a consequence of mergers in the press which were mainly due to economic factors.

Net advertising sales for Switzerland (million CHF.)

Net advertising sales excluding production costs	2005	2006	2007	±% 06/07
Daily press	1'232	1'272	1'341	5,5
Regional weekly press	212	229	222	–2,8
Sunday press	171	188	202	7,3
Total for daily/weekly/Sunday press	**1'615**	**1'688**	**1'765**	**4,6**
Including press titles sold/subscribed to	1'357	1'391	1'449	4,2
Including press titles free of charge	258	298	316	6,2
General-interest press	226	223	239	7,2
Financial and commercial press	68	67	76	13,3
Special and hobby magazines	257	263	281	7,1
Technical publications	133	128	126	–2,2
Total for press	**2'299**	**2'369**	**2'487**	**5,0**
Television (incl. sponsoring)	588	615	637	3,6
Radio (incl. sponsoring)	142	138	136	–1,1
Cinema	37	37	33	–9,6
Teletext	10	8	9	13,8
Total for electronic media	**777**	**797**	**815**	**2,3**
External advertising	559	598	663	10,9
Address books	209	211	206	–2,0
Trade fairs and exhibitions	257	345	385	11,5,
Direct advertising (distribution costs)	1'275	1'313	1'307	–0,4
Total for other media	**2'300**	**2'466**	**2'562**	**3,9**
Total value	**5'376**	**5'632**	**5'864**	**4,1**
Internet (MediaFocus)[1]	36	47	52	10,9

Source: Swiss Institute of Advertising Statistics. [1] Only traditional online advertising

The new media house of Radio e Televisiun Rumantscha (RTR) was opened in Chur in 2006. RTR is the only electronic media company to provide a public service for the Svizra rumantscha, one of the four linguistic regions of Switzerland. A 14-hour radio programme and 90 minutes of television a week inform and entertain the Rhaeto-Romanics extensively in their mother tongue.

Following the regional realignments of the 1990s, the "St. Galler Tagblatt" and the "Südostschweiz" have achieved dominance in the eastern parts of the country while in central Switzerland the "Neue Luzerner Zeitung" and in the Canton of Argovia the "Mittelland Zeitung" have come to the fore. Other major media houses in German-speaking Switzerland are Tamedia that publishes the "Tages-Anzeiger" and the Basler Mediengruppe with the "Basler Zeitung". In western Switzerland, the Edipresse group based in Lausanne has a clear lead with its series of newspapers "Le Temps", "Le Matin", "24 heures" and the "Tribune de Genève". On the long contested Bernese market the two dailies "Berner Zeitung" and "Bund" merged in 2003: two largely autonomous and independent editorial departments work under the umbrella of Espace Media, the advertising columns being common to both.

Switzerland's largest daily newspaper is the small format free tabloid, "20 Minuten". In just a few years, it has achieved a circulation of 530'000 copies. It is distributed at points in larger towns where large streams of commuters regularly pass in the mornings.

The same is true of "Le Matin Bleu" (230'000 copies), the first French language free newspaper, which was launched in 2005 by Lausanne's Edipresse, Just four months later, Zurich-based Tamedia launched another free newspaper for the French-speaking region with "20 minutes" (220'000). Behind this come the tabloid newspaper "Blick" (230'000 copies), the Zurich "Tages-Anzeiger" (213'000), the "Berner Zeitung" (212'000) and the "Mittelland Zeitung" (202'000). The first 'traditional' French language title appears in 14th position with "24 heures" (86'000).

Alongside the freesheets, Sunday newspapers are becoming more and more popular; since 2002 there have been three Sunday newspapers in German-speaking Switzerland: the "Sonntagsblick" (Ringier), the "Sonntagszeitung" (Tamedia) and the "NZZ am Sonntag". Ringier is also represented in Ticino with its "Il Caffé" Sunday publication. The popular Edipresse title "Matin Dimanche" is published in western Switzerland.

Sunday has become a popular media day: major political and industrial figures are keen to have interviews published in the

Sunday press, high circulation figures being both to their advantage and that of the publishers.

The two biggest magazines in Switzerland are the two consumer magazines "Beobachter" (310'000 copies) and "K-Tipp" (270'000), followed by the "Schweizer Illustrierte" (210'000). In Switzerland, the debate surrounding quality in journalism has become more heated over the past few years. Swiss readers are turning more frequently to the Swiss Press Council. It is supported by journalists' associations and serves the general public and people working in the media as a complaints board for ethical questions concerning the media and regularly pronounces on controversial publications.

www.presserat.ch

Radio, television and multimedia

The majority of the Swiss people obtain their TV programmes via the cable networks. As regards cable net density, Switzerland is Europe's peak group. Over 85% of Swiss households are connected to cable, which gives them access to at least 50 radio and television programmes. However, more and more programmes can only be received digitally, with the attendant additional costs. Very few of the three million or so viewing households are dependent on terrestrial transmission. The Federal Constitution empowers the Confederation to enact legislation for the regulation of radio and television. **www.bakom.ch** The Confederation also has to ensure through its mandate the media's independence and freedom as to choice of programme content. The Radio and Television Law (RTVG) defines programming. Swiss media policy provides radio and television in all four languages. There is at present one private full-time television channel, 3+, broadcasting throughout Switzerland alongside established broadcaster SRG SSR idée suisse. Up to now, several attempts to establish commercial regional language channels in competition have failed due to the smallness of the markets and to problematic programming and financing concepts. Nevertheless, Switzerland possesses at least 40 local and regional television channels which broadcast regional news on a modest scale. Specialised programmes in

"Weatherman" Thomas Bucheli and his colleagues present DRS Swiss Television's weather forecast "Meteo" all year around from the roof of the television studio.

Consumer topics attract large audiences on Swiss television. Western Switzerland's TSR television's programme "A Bon Entendeur" has been uncovering deplorable situations for years, which are then frequently taken up on a national scale by other media. The programme is presented by Manuelle Pernoud.

the area of film and music have been established in various linguistic regions. The revision of the RTVG is extending the advertising opportunities of the commercial channels and allows them to share the fee income of the SRG SSR idée suisse. At present, some 50 local and regional commercial radio channels have a broadcasting licence. In addition, satellite and cable networks transmitting programmes from numerous foreign television stations have achieved up to 60 per cent of the 24-hour market share alongside SRG SSR. SRG SSR idée suisse holds a federal broadcasting concession but, as a national and regional organisation, is obliged to produce and broadcast radio and television programmes in all four national languages. In doing this, SRG SSR idée suisse must take into consideration the cultural and ethnic diversity of Switzerland (public service). SRG SSR is not a state-owned but a privately owned organisation operating as a public service. It works on commercial principles, but is non-profit making. An independent complaints authority (UBI), backed by the government and the radio and television programme providers, has

been in existence since 1984 to rule on programme complaints. **www.ubi.admin.ch** The SRG SSR offers multilingual programmes nationally and in many different media. It comprises 8 television and 18 radio programmes in the four national languages, complementary websites in a total of ten languages and teletext in German, French and Italian. The content ranges from news, reports and background reports relating to politics, culture, society and sport to entertainment with feature films, sitcoms, radio plays, shows, talk shows and music. The SRG SSR's programmes can be received nationally, but are tailored above all to the needs of the audience in the various linguistic regions of Switzerland.

In contrast to the strong foreign competition, the Swiss content makes the SRG SSR idée suisse unique and indispensable. Foreign competitors have little interest in offering Swiss content – with just a few exceptions: for example advertising slots and football broadcasts on Sat 1. **www.srgssrideesuisse.ch**

The offering from Swissinfo/Swiss Radio International (SRI) is targeted at Swiss citizens living abroad and an international audience with an interest in Switzerland. The internet information platform **www.swissinfo.ch** offers news and information on Switzerland in the form of text, pictures, sound and video contributions in nine languages (German, French, Italian, English, Spanish, Portuguese, Arabic, Chinese and Japanese). Priority is given to information from the areas of politics, economics, culture and science and technology. In addition, SRG SSR is a joint programme contributor to the German-language collaborative programme 3 Sat, the French-language collaborative programme TV 5 and to Arte. It also produces contributions for specialist TV channels such as Eurosport, Euronews and CNN.

www.swissinfo.ch,

www.swissworld.org

Two thirds of SRG's production and transmission costs for radio and television programmes are covered by the broadcast reception licence (CHF 38,50 per household per month) and one third by advertising and sponsorship money. Compared to other European countries the licence fees are high. However, judging by the broad range of programmes and the high income

per capita, Switzerland is about average with its fees.

SRG SSR makes programmes for a small market which is divided up into four languages for over seven million people. It is only thanks to the mixture of finance from fee income and commercial receipts that it is able to offer programmes that can compete at international level.

SRG's annual turnover is CHF 1,5 billion. Its workforce in Switzerland is around 6'000 employees. Around 3 million radio and television reception licences are issued in Switzerland. Advertising is allowed on SRG SSR television programmes but forbidden on its radio programmes. Sponsoring is permitted on both media. The legal status of the SRG SSR is a union of associations. This union forms the supporting organisation of SRG SSR idée Suisse. It acts as a bridge between the public and the company. Its members hold an influence over SRG SSR in the same way as shareholders influence a joint stock company.

Switzerland's special topography means that it is more difficult providing it with television and radio transmitters than other countries. Therefore, a large number of households have cable TV.

MASS SPORT AND TOP RESULTS

Tennis star Roger Federer is world-famous, as is the 2008 Olympic men's cycling time trial gold medallist Fabian Cancellara. In the last few years, the national football team has attracted attention beyond the national borders as well. In addition, Switzerland is a country of mass sports, with skiing, hiking, Schwingen (a form of wrestling), Hornussen (a cross between baseball and golf, also called "Baseball Swiss style"), football, mountain biking, swimming, skating and numerous other sports being popular. According to a representative survey, three out of every four people follow the national and international sports events in the media. Important international sports federations have their headquarters in Switzerland. Not least of all, sport is an important economic factor.

www.swissworld.org

Hiking, mountain biking and team sport

Two out of every three Swiss nationals take part in sport at least once a week. The country's sports associations hold more than 400'000 sports events every year. The majority, roughly 320'000, of these are league matches in team sports, with 170'000 alone being football matches. On average, each team match attracts approximately one hundred spectators, with on average forty people being actively involved in the match and roughly twenty people on the touchline looking after the players, preparing for the match and being responsible for clearing up.

One of the most popular sporting activities in Switzerland is hiking, which is becoming a fashionable sport and increasingly being referred to as trekking. More than 60 per cent of the population go hiking at least once a year. Whether sprightly senior citizens, young families or sporty walkers – all appreciate the dense, well-maintained Swiss network of footpaths, with more than 50'000 kilometres being marked. The footpaths featuring signposts with exact details of places and times lead to a wide variety of destinations and a wide range of experiences: the markings and signposts of the easy footpaths in the Mittelland and the foothills of the Alps are "yellow", while "white-red-white" is used in Alpine country and for demanding routes. "White-blue-white" indicates the direction through the ice and snow, right up to the highest peaks. Volunteers are mainly responsible for maintaining the hiking trails.

Hiking is also an important backbone of Swiss tourism. This has always been the case for summer and autumn, but more and more people are also discovering the winter landscape on foot thanks to a wide and varied range of prepared winter trails. Snowshoes are also becoming increasingly popular and many more routes are being signed for them as well.
www.swisshiking.ch (Swiss hiking trails)
www.wandersite.ch

The marked cycle routes are also being continually extended throughout the whole of Switzerland as well as specially signed trails for mountain bikers and inline skaters. Riders can enjoy tranquil rides on the many bridlepaths or take part in competitions. Highlights are the races – including betting on the horses – in Schachen in Argovia, in the rural style at the Marché Concours in Saignelégier and in winter on the frozen lake in chic St. Moritz.

The Vita-Parcours (Vita courses) sprang up in Swiss forests at a time before everybody was talking about fitness and wellness. Created by a life assurance company, the aim was to promote mobility, stamina and strength among the population by means of simple exercises on circular trails. Each course is made up of 15 posts with various exercises. At each post an information panel clearly explains the exercise and recommends how often or how long it should be carried out, depending on age and condition. Approximately 20 per cent of the population regularly use the more than 500 Vita-Parcours. **www.vitaparcours.ch**

Football: Number 1 sport

Football fascinates the masses in Switzerland as well. No other sport is at the same time such a popular sport, an economic factor and a mass phenomenon. The Swiss Football League numbers approximately 250'000 active participants – roughly five per cent of them women. Many others are enthusiastically involved in corporate sport or take part in one or more of the countless hobby tournaments which are held the length and breadth of the country in the warm season. Swiss professional football

Sport as a living national tradition: Schwingen (a type of wrestling) is a famous trial of strength. Throughout the summer, strong lads pit their strength against each other in a sawdust ring in the Swiss national sport. The winner is the one who leaves his opponent on his back. Wrestling competitions are a firm part of many mountain and alpine festivals.
Left: An advertisement for top-class Swiss sport: Roger Federer, international tennis champion (Picture Roger Federer Management).

Ice hockey is enthusiastically followed in Switzerland. The annual Spengler Cup (the picture shows Davos vs. Team Canada) in Davos attracts the masses. ZSC Lions of Zurich were the first winners of the Champions Hockey League in 2008/2009. In April 2009, Switzerland hosted the Ice Hockey World Championship.

plays a rather minor role compared with other European countries, as none of the teams is able to match the top teams of the European leagues, either financially or in terms of sporting achievements. Despite this, individual clubs such as FC Basel manage to qualify, time and time again, for at least the group phase of the Champions League. **www.football.ch**

The Swiss U21, U20 and U19 national men's and women's junior football teams have repeatedly succeeded in qualifying for World and European Championships and have achieved some impressive results. Professional Swiss footballers are also increasingly playing for the top European clubs. EURO 08, which was hosted jointly by Switzerland and Austria, represented the Swiss national team's last major appearance on a European stage. However, to the fans' regret, both of the host countries were knocked out in the first round of the final tournament. Huge media coverage prompted the announcement of the new national team coach in the summer of 2008: Ottmar Hitzfeld, whose last job was as coach at FC Bayern Munich, is one of the most successful coaches in football. **www.euro2008.com**

Olympics and other major events

The Winter Olympics have been held in Switzerland twice – in 1924 and 1948, both times in St. Moritz in the Engadine. World and European Championships in a very wide range of sports are held in Switzerland much more frequently. The venues include famous winter sports locations for Alpine skiing and Nordic skiing, the forests of the Mittelland for orienteering and large towns and cities for indoor handball. Switzerland regularly wins medals and finishes in the top places in competitions, whether at home or abroad – frequently in the well-known sports and even more frequently in the so-called peripheral sports or in new disciplines.

Switzerland has enjoyed and is still enjoying a great deal of success in winter sport, with the skiers having been particularly used to success up to the 1990's. In 1994, Vreni Schneider won a complete set of Olympic medals at the Winter Olympics in Lillehammer. Today, snowboarders such as the brothers Philipp and Simon Schoch, Tanja Frieden and Daniela Meuli win lots of medals. Swiss nationals are also successful in curling, and the bobsleigh team has brought home medals from virtually all of the Winter Olympics up to now.

Switzerland has won a total of 305 medals – 86 gold medals, 110 silver and 109 bronze medals at the Olympics between 1896 and 2008. The number of Swiss World Champions is several times higher – so high that there are no statistics.

www.swissolympic.ch

Paralympic Games

Swiss sportsmen and sportswomen with a physical handicap are outstanding internationally. They do exceptionally well both at the Paralympics, the Olympic Games for disability sport, and at the World and European Championships.

The many sports include wheelchair racing by paraplegics and tetraplegics, the long jump by leg amputees and skiing without arms. The Swiss Sports Association for the Disabled lists the world champion titles; since 1982 there have been 129, for instance in Nordic skiing or downhill skiing, in track and field athletics, archery, weight-lifting, table tennis or water-skiing. The para-

Swiss Medals at the Olympic Games 1896 to 2008

Summer Olympics

Sport	Gold	Silver	Bronze	Total
Beach volleyball	0	0	1	1
Canoeing	0	1	0	1
Cycling	3	6	7	16
Equestrian	4	10	7	21
Fencing	1	4	3	8
Football	0	1	0	1
Gymnastics	16	19	13	48
Handball	0	0	1	1
Judo	1	1	2	4
Rowing	6	8	9	23
Sailing	1	1	1	3
Shooting	6	6	8	20
Swimming	0	0	1	1
Tennis	2	0	0	2
Track and field athletics	0	6	2	8
Triathlon	1	0	2	3
Weight-lifting	0	2	2	4
Wrestling	4	4	6	14
Total for Summer Olympics	**45**	**69**	**65**	**179**

Special competitions	Gold	Silver	Bronze	Total
Aeronautical prize	1	0	0	1
Architecture	1	1	0	2
Art competition	1	2	0	3
Commercial art	0	1	1	2
Mountaineer prize	1	0	0	1
Total for special competitions	**4**	**4**	**1**	**9**

Winter Olympics

Sport	Gold	Silver	Bronze	Total
Alpine skiing	16	19	18	53
Bobsleigh	9	10	11	30
Cross-country skiing	0	0	4	4
Curling	1	2	1	4
Freestyle skiing	2	0	1	3
Ice hockey	0	0	2	2
Ice-skating	0	2	1	3
Nordic combined	1	2	1	4
Skeleton	1	0	2	3
Ski jumping	2	1	0	3
Snowboarding	5	1	2	8
Total for Winter Olympics	**37**	**37**	**43**	**117**

Source: Swissolympic

In 2006 the Swiss Disabled Sports Association celebrated its fiftieth anniversary. A further organisation, the Swiss Paralympic Committee, is responsible for top-class sport. It offers physically handicapped and visually impaired athletes financial, material and organisational support to allow them to participate in the Summer and Winter Paralympic Games and World and European Championships.
Pictured: Marcel Hug, athlete in several disciplines, multiple medal winner at the 2004 Summer Paralympics in Athens and at the 2005 European Championships in Espoo as well as five-times 2006 World Champion at the Junior World Championships in Dublin.

plegic Heinz Frei stands out in particular with 26 gold, 21 silver and 16 bronze medals between 1986 and 1998. The tetraplegic Giuseppe Forni enjoyed similar success during the same period. He won 19 gold, six silver and ten bronze medals in running disciplines from the 100 m sprint up to marathon distance. The blind skier Natacha Chevalley skied to ten victories at the World Championships from 1990 to 1996.
www.swissparalympic.ch
www.plusport.ch (Switzerland Disability Sport)

The major names in Swiss sport

The professional tennis players Roger Federer and Martina Hingis are known all over the world. For a long time number 1 in the world tennis rankings, Federer won the All England Championships at Wimbledon for the fifth consecutive time in July 2007, making him and Björn Borg (1976-80) the only players to have achieved this. His five back-to-back victories at the U.S. Open (2004-2008) are unparalleled. Federer's achievements in recent years led to him being voted World Sportsman of the Year in 2005, 2006, 2007 and 2008. The major

greats in sport also include Simone Niggli-Luder, ten times World Champion in orienteering, and Ernesto Bertarelli who, with his team, brought home the America's Cup, the most prestigious trophy for sailors, to Switzerland in 2003 and 2007. Since then sailing has become more popular in Switzerland. Sportsmen such as Roger Federer or the motorcycle racer Tom Lüthi, who became World Champion of the 125cc class at the age of just nineteen years old, serve as role models for many young people. While a good many sporting successes only last a little while, other athletes remain at the top for years. For example, the gymnast Georges Miez won Olympic gold five times, silver three times and one bronze medal between 1924 and 1936. The dressage rider Henri Chammartin is still unsurpassed: he won a gold, a silver and two bronze medals between 1952 and 1968 at the Olympics. The ski racer Marie-Theres Nadig confirmed her surprise 1972 gold medal with an Olympic bronze in 1980. She went on to become trainer of the national skiing team. Like her, others have also built their professional or personal successes on a sports career such as, for example, Ferdy Kübler – known as Ferdy "National" – a professional cyclist for many years, or Bernhard Russi, who still appears on television today thanks to his downhill skiing victories in the seventies. Karl Molitor was awarded Olympic silver in the alpine combination and bronze in the downhill in 1948 and won the Lauberhorn ski race eleven times, before he manufactured top-class ski boots for many years. Roger Staub, Olympic gold medallist in the giant slalom in 1960, is still well-known thanks to a practical winter sports aid: thousands still protect themselves today against driving snow and the cold with the Roger Staub balaclava. Finally, Markus Ryffel went from being the 5'000m silver medallist at Los Angeles in 1984 to a running trainer for half the nation.

A good many devote themselves to top-class sport and professional training or study at the same time. Some of them make a name for themselves years later in politics or economics. For instance, two former top-class handball players became a Federal Councillor and Deputy Director-General of the Swiss radio and television company, SRG SSR idée Suisse, respectively.

The first national elite sports school in Kreuzlingen is further promoting the link between a good education and the highest sporting achievements. It is the only upper secondary school in Switzerland to bear the title of Swiss Olympic Sport School.

Sport, international understanding, politics

Sport is an ideal way to open doors: sport can be used to establish contacts, develop and integrate activities, impart values and break up conflicts. Sport helps to promote a culture of peaceful opposition. Sport in general and football in particular are considered to unite people in Switzerland as well. Sport is a social factor – it brings people together: many sons of immigrant foreign workers are actively involved with native children and young people in the junior sections of the numerous Swiss football clubs. Several of them display a great deal of talent and are challenged and encouraged. Quite a few of them have become a popular mainstay of the Swiss national team thanks to their footballing skills.

Snowboarding is particularly fashionable with the young. Swiss athletes regularly achieve top-class results in top-class sport and, therefore, in the still relatively new Olympic discipline. Daniela Meuli (pictured), five-times World Cup season winner in the snowboarding parallel giant slalom, also won gold at the 2006 Winter Olympics in Turin. (Picture Swiss-Ski)

Quite frequently, top Swiss sportsmen and women win coveted titles in peripheral sports. Maya Pedersen-Bieri (pictured) is considered to be the most successful skeleton athlete since ladies have competed in this sport. In 2005 she became World Skeleton Champion and she won the gold medal at the 2006 Winter Olympics in Turin.

When the UN expressly stated that sport should be used to foster international understanding and as a means to promote education, health, development and peace a few years ago, the former Swiss Federal Councillor Adolf Ogi became the UN's first special adviser on sport.

International sports federations

As a neutral country with a good infrastructure, Switzerland is the headquarters of many umbrella sports organisations. The International Olympic Committee (IOC) is located in Lausanne and also includes a large sports museum. In the same city the Court of Arbitration for Sport has settled approximately 200 disputes a year from all sports since 1984 as the court of highest instance. The Fédération Internationale de Football Association (FIFA), the International Ice Hockey Federation, the International Rowing Federation and the International Aeronautical Federation are also domiciled in Switzerland. It is hardly surprising that the International Ski Federation is based in Switzerland. On the other hand, what may be surprising is that the

Fédération Internationale de l'Automobile also has its headquarters in Switzerland, even though Formula 1 and other circuit racing have been banned in Switzerland since 1955.

In addition, the World Anti-Doping Agency (WADA), which was established in 1999, has its headquarters in Switzerland. Created by the IOC, the WADA works for doping-free sport. The foundation which is governed by Swiss law is supervised by the Confederation. The WADA code of conduct is increasingly being adopted in international treaties and is therefore being declared to be mandatory in more and more countries.

Sport as an economic factor

Today, wide sections of sport are dominated by huge and costly financial expenditure in terms of equipment and training and are being increasingly commercialised, and this is not just the case in Switzerland. Sport sales are estimated to be six to ten billion francs for Switzerland. According to a survey, each person taking part in sport in Switzerland spends approximately 1'400 francs a year on his/her hobby. In addition, there is the income connected with the events: merchandising, food, advertising, televisions rights, etc.

The increasing importance of top-class sport as an economic factor and the numerous active sport clubs in Switzerland have led to multifunctional football stadiums being built in many places, the most famous of which are St. Jakobspark in Basle, the former Wankdorf and now Stade de Suisse in Berne, the Maladière in Neuchâtel and the Charmilles in Geneva. These venues generally play host to football matches once a week, with other sports, concerts, performances, shopping and restaurant visits being the order of the day the rest of the time. All kinds of other uses of the ancillary rooms provide the stadium operators with additional income. For example, the extensive and modern infrastructure in Switzerland is increasingly being used by foreign sports clubs and teams for training.

Prizes for sports architecture

Not only does Switzerland boast excellent sportsmen and women, but it also has architects who design excellent sports venues. For example, Basle's St. Jakob football stadium was built according to the designs of Herzog & De Meuron. In addition, these two renowned architects are responsible for what was one of the highlights of the 2008 Olympics in Peking, the central stadium for the track and field athletics events. Called the "Bird's nest", the project has succeeded in striking a superb balance between contemporary architectural language and the Chinese mentality with its transparent, filigree structure. The stadium cost around 500 million francs. Jacques Herzog and Philippe de Meuron have prominent predecessors: as long ago as 1912, Swiss architects Eugène Edouard Monod and Alphonse Laverrière won a gold medal for their stadium for the Summer Olympics in Stockholm.

The last few years have seen the construction, in Switzerland, of several new football stadiums designed by famous architects. These include, for example, St. Jakob-Park in Basle, Maladière in Neuchâtel, Charmilles in Geneva and the Stade de Suisse in Berne (pictured), on which Lausanne's internationally renowned architect, Rodolphe Luscher, collaborated.

Entry into the Confederation	1291 Uri	1291 Schwyz	1291 Nidwalden
1291 Obwalden	1332 Lucerne	1351 Zurich
1352 Glarus	1352 Zug	1353 Berne
1481 Fribourg	1481 Solothurn	1501 Basle-Town
1501 Basle-Country	1501 Schaffhausen	1513 Appenzell Outer-Rhodes
1513 Appenzell Inner-Rhodes	1803 St. Gall	1803 Grisons
1803 Argovia	1803 Thurgovia	1803 Ticino
1803 Vaud	1815 Valais	1815 Neuchâtel
1815 Geneva	1979 Jura	

Published by the Federal Department of Foreign Affairs, General Secretariat, Presence Switzerland. **www.eda.admin.ch**
Presence Switzerland promotes an authentic image of modern Switzerland worldwide. **www.image-switzerland.ch**

Editing: Hallwag Kümmerly+Frey and Presence Switzerland

Project and Editing Coordination: Media Impression, Schweiz, Lorenz Beer

Translation: Team Übersetzer Tanner & Creola, Oberwangen

Design/cartography: Hallwag Kümmerly+Frey, wa.zwei.werbeagentur

Printing: Printed in Switzerland

Overall production: Hallwag Kümmerly+Frey AG, 3322 Schönbühl-Berne
Presence Switzerland, 3003 Berne

Picture record

Front cover: Parliament Building and Parliament Square, Berne
Contents: www.admin.ch, Archaeological Service of the Canton of Lucerne, Archeodunu Avenches, Bildlupe/Renate Wernli, www.bilaterale.ch, Birdlife of Switzerland/Emile Barbelette, Council of Europe, Centre Dürrenmatt, www.duttiderriese.ch, Entlebuch Biosphere Reserve, Federal Chancellery, Federal Department of Defence, Civil Protectic and Sports (DDPS), Federal Department of Economic Affairs (DEA), Federal Customs Administration (FCA), Einsiedeln Tourism, Stephan Engler, Roger Federer Management Föhn Theaterproduktion, Fribourg Tourism, Geneva Tourism, Grisons Holidays, Karl-Hei Hug, Keystone, Lake Geneva Region Tourist Office, Lake Lucerne Shipping Company, Lucerne Festival, Mendrisio Tourism, Novartis, www.parlament.ch, M. Pedersen-Bieri, Pro Natura, SBB, Ernst Scheidegger (© NZZ/Pro Litteris), ONUART Foundation and Antonia and Augusti TORRES, Paul Klee Centre, Jakob Schlaepfer, Franz Schwendimai Christof Sonderegger, SRG/SSR idée suisse, Swiss Agency for Development and Cooperation (SDC), Swisscom, Swiss Federal Institute for Snow and Avalanche Researc Swiss Federal Institute of Technology of Zurich (ETH), Swiss Festival of Traditional Costumes and Alpine Herdsmen "Unspunnen", Swiss Fire Brigade Association, Swiss-Image, www.swissimage.ch-Andy Mettler, Swiss Milk Producers, Swiss National Museu Swiss National Park, Swiss Picture Base, Swiss Post, Swiss Red Cross (SRC), Swiss Schwingen Association (Swiss wrestling), Switzerland Tourism, www.swissfilms.ch, Swi paralympic/Peter Läuppi, Swiss-Ski, Ticino Tourism, TSR, Vaud Tourism, The Swiss Museum of Transport and Communication,VOtth, Zurich Opera House/Peter Schnetz.